Treatise of Revolutionary Psychology

David, a symbol of the Essence, lifts aloft the head
of the conquered Goliath: the ego.
ENGRAVING BY GUSTAVE DORÉ.

Treatise of Revolutionary Psychology

Samael Aun Weor

Glorian Publishing
PO Box 209
Clinton, CT 06413 USA
glorian.org

A translation of *Tratado de Psicología Revolucionária,* 1974.

Library of Congress Cataloging-in-Publication Data

Names: סמאל און ואור, Samael Aun Weor, 1917-1977, author.

Title: Treatise of Revolutionary Psychology / Conceived and
   written by Samael Aun Weor; translated and edited by
   Glorian Publishing.

Identifiers: LCCN 2024934851 (print)

Subjects: LCSH: Psychology

Classification: LCC BF1-990

LC record available at: https://lccn.loc.gov/2024934851

ISBN 978-1-934206-76-8

Glorian Publishing books are printed on acid-free paper
and meet the guidelines for permanence and durability of
the Production Guidelines for Book Longevity of the Coun-
cil on Library Resources.

Printed in the United States of America.

Glorian Publishing is a non-profit organization. All
proceeds go to further the distribution of these books. For
more information, visit glorian.org

Contents

Introduction

I have written this book in order for you to study it. Please read it carefully; I have written it for you...

Indeed, to know how to read is something very difficult. To read a newspaper is easy, yet this book is different.

Commonly, when we are reading, there is a translator inside of us: the "I," the ego,[1] the "myself" that translates everything according to its own concepts, ideas, opinions, etc. Therefore, to know how to read is not something very easy.

It is necessary to understand that within us there is something other than just the physical body. We have a body of flesh and bones; this is obvious. Everyone can accept this fact. However, only a few can understand that we have a psychology[2] that can be modified.

---

1   From the Latin for "I" and similar to the Greek Εγώ. In esotericism, the term ego is very different from the Freudian definition. In practical spirituality, the term ego refers to psychological constructs in the mind that trap the consciousness. See glossary.

2   From Greek psyche (pskhe) meaning "soul," and Logos, the "principle governing the

If we really want transformation, we have to understand this psychology.

Those who accept the existence of their own psychology, obviously begin to self-observe. When someone self-observes, it is a signal that one is trying to achieve self-transformation. We need self-transformation.

Life as it is, indeed, is not very attractive. To be born, grow up, grow old, and o die are all something very boring. To work in order to exist and to exist in a psychologically miserable way is worthless.

It is not only those who have money who live in a psychologically miserable manner, but as well, those who do not. This is because there are two ways to wallow in the mud: in the mud of misery and in the mud of wealth. Both ways are psychologically degrading. Therefore, to live in either manner, to exist without a reason, not knowing why and for what, is to live without a psychological purpose.

---

cosmos," the Word, God. True psychology is "the knowledge of the relationship of the soul with God." Esoteric psychology is the highest and most potent level of that knowledge, and is entered into in levels, according to the internal, initiatic process of the seeker.

What are we? What is the reason for our existence? What do we live for? So many problems and in the end, what?

Each one of us is just a machine that transforms energies... It so happens that the energies of the planets, the planetary energies of our solar system, cannot pass directly into our planet. This is because our planet is different; it is a world governed by 48 laws,[3] a completely different world than the other worlds of our solar system.

Looking at the planets from this viewpoint, it is obvious that this solar system needs channels in order to allow the passing of the cosmic or universal energies directly into the layers of our planetary organism. It is not enough to allow the energies to pass. The energies need to be transformed through many channels. Thus, only a transformed and adapted energy can be useful to the planet Earth.

Let us take into account that the Earth is a living organism that needs to exist, and that needs cosmic energies in order to do so. Therefore, as we need energies in

---

3   To learn about these laws, read *The Elimination of Satan's Tail* by Samael Aun Weor.

order to exist, in the same way the Earth needs energy in order to exist and live.

Yet, the energies that the Earth receives for its existence come from other planets of our solar system. I repeat: because our planet is different from other planets, the energy has to be transformed in order to be used to feed our planet Earth. This energy cannot be transformed if there are no channels to pass it through.

Fortunately, these channels exist. They were made by the Sun, and they are the organic life, which as a thin skin was established in the terrestrial layer by the Logos.[4]

Therefore, the thin skin of organic life formed by plants, animals and humans is necessary in order to allow the energy to be transformed and to pass into the inner layers of the Earth. Only in that manner can the Earth exist; otherwise it cannot exist as a living organism.

Therefore, we, as humanoids, are just simple machines through which cosmic energy has to pass. Each one of us receives certain charges of electricity and magne-

---

4   Greek, "word." A symbolic reference to divinity. See glossary.

tism that are unconsciously transformed
and retransmitted automatically into the
inner layers of the Earth. This is the only
reason for our existence.

Behold how much bitterness there is
in order to just let our Earth, our planet,
live and rotate around the Sun. We feel
so great, when indeed we are just simple,
small energy-transforming machines.
Thus, the reason for our existence is just
that: to allow this planet to exist. This is
the reason for our small lives... Unhappy
days... To work in order to eat, to exist just
because of Nature's necessity.

Therefore, Nature does not care about
our ideas nor our beliefs. All that Nature
wants is to receive the necessary food, the
energetic food, that has to pass through
our bodies. That is all.

But, behold how we live! Yelling at
home or in the streets, suffering under the
weight of a tyrant in the factory or in the
office, paying our taxes in order to exist
as citizens, paying the rent, etc. Absolutely
all of this is just so that this planet can
exist, so that it can be part of the conjunction of worlds, so that it can be alive.

So many mothers who suffer, so many
teenagers who do not have enough money

to live, so many mothers who do not even have milk to feed their babies. So many elders with their experiences of life, so many children that are beginning to receive taunts, all of them exist in order for this planet to be alive.

This truth is hard and cruel, or better if I say pitiless; yet, we are that, and nothing else. If at least we were human beings, then we would be something; but we are not even that. We are just poor intellectual animals,[5] carrying the sadness of our existence. Yes, intellectual animals is what we are. This may seem very pessimistic.

When experiencing celebration, we think that life has its happy moments; but this is because we do not know what happiness really is. We confuse moments of pleasure with authentic and legitimate happiness. Obviously, we are walking on an erroneous path.

What is that which remains after pleasure? Only disillusions and deception! How many times has a man and a woman who think they are in love get married and later realize that they were

---

5   The current condition of humanity: animals with intellect. See glossary.

just fascinated. That was not love; they thought that it was love, but it was not. Love was confused with passion. So, once the animal passion is satisfied, what remains in that couple is the loathing, the saturation, the deception. That is all. Afterwards, everything becomes a routine. They speak only of bank accounts, rent, the clothes that need to be washed, that they need breakfast on time to go to work, etc. Sometimes we take a walk in order to find an escape from the boredom, or we go to a party and we end up in a huge drunken state.

Thus, in this way life is passing by until the moment that we become old. Once we are elders, we feel like veterans. We enjoy the calls of our grandchildren; we enjoy being called "grandpa, grandma" and we like to tell the tales of our sad experiences (which we feel very proud about). Our life is filled with comments like, "In my time, the president did this and that, etc." We recount our fights, about the battles that we participated in, and we possibly even display our wounds of war that make us feel proud... Just sadness! The usual conversations, "Our brother has died," "Our cousin lost his fortune,"

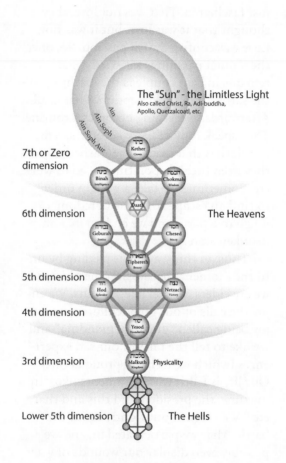

The "Sun" - the Limitless Light
Also called Christ, Ra, Adi-buddha, Apollo, Quetzalcoatl, etc.

Ain
Ain Soph
Ain Soph Aur

7th or Zero
dimension

כתר
Kether
Crown

בינה
Binah
Intelligence

חכמה
Chokmah
Wisdom

Daath

6th dimension

The Heavens

גבורה
Geburah
Justice

חסד
Chesed
Mercy

תפארת
Tiphereth
Beauty

5th dimension

הוד
Hod
Splendor

נצח
Netzach
Victory

4th dimension

יסוד
Yesod
Foundation

3rd dimension

מלכות
Malkuth
Kingdom

Physicality

Lower 5th dimension

The Hells

KABBALAH, THE TREE OF LIFE

or "Those times were better," etc. Thus, in the end death comes... So the outcome of our unhappy life is death. This is what we get after having worked and suffered so much!

Fortunately, the Sun[6] is compassionate. Something secret exists within its creation; this is also truth. So, the Sun has created this humanity as simple small machines that help its creation. That is Nature, but it is also true that the Sun wants to create something else.

The Logos does not create this Nature, it does not create organic life in a world that moves around the Sun just for diversion, without a logical goal. It would not be logical to have created this planet for nothing. To create something without a goal would be the absurdity of absurdities. I think that not even you would do it. You would not create an invention and suffer for it, spend a life for it, and later destroy it. Therefore, you must understand that this creation has an objective.

---

6 The giver and supporter of life, which in all religions symbolizes the universal cosmic Christ. Christ is the basis of every religion. Each religion has their own symbols and names for Christ. See glossary.

The solar intelligence charges a price for the creation of the thin skin of organic life upon the face of the Earth. The solar intelligence wants to get something from it; it has an interest in it.

The goal of the solar intelligence is to obtain a harvest of solar human beings. The idea is not bad at all; yet, it is difficult. It is, indeed, a tremendous and hard experiment in the test tube of Nature. This is what the solar intelligence wants: to create solar human beings.

Diogenes and his lamp comes into my mind in this moment. One day, Diogenes walked through the streets of Athens with a lamp in his hand trying to find a true man, yet he could not find one. He looked in the houses, rooms, corridors, and yards of the wise citizens of Athens... "What are you looking for, Diogenes?" they all asked him.

"A human..!" Diogenes answered.

"The streets and the public forums are full of humans!" they said.

He answered, "Those are not human, they are beasts, since they eat, sleep and live as beasts!" To that end, he visited the homes of scientists, artists, and every-where he was doing the same thing. It is obvious that he was making more and more enemies as he was visiting their homes. Everybody ended up feeling very offended by Diogenes...

Yet, he was right: he did not find a single human! Many wanted to believe that he found one somewhere. The followers of Marat thought that he had found one in a cave, and that it was Marat. Absurd! The truth is that he did not find any human. If Marat was a human, good for him, yet to find a real human (a solar human being) is indeed difficult.

Diogenes lived in a barrel, and there he ate and slept; he did not even have a house. It is stated that before Diogenes died, he was visited by Alexander the Great. Alexander was the one who put Europe and Asia under his rule. So, a simple man like Diogenes who lived in a barrel even threw out Alexander the Great.

Alexander found Diogenes lying in the sun in agony. When Diogenes saw so much company near him, he raised himself a little and vouchsafed to look upon Alexander. When Alexander kindly asked him whether he wanted anything, Diogenes said, "Yes, I would prefer that you not stand between me and my Sun (that is to say, between him and his inner God)." Alexander was so struck at this answer that he did not have any other choice than to just go away. A humble man like Diogenes threw out Alexander the Great. This is something that not everyone can do; is it not so?

Authentic humans, true human beings in the most complete sense of the word, are very hard to find.

Fortunately, the Sun has deposited in the sexual glands the seed needed in order to create the authentic human. This seed could develop if we were to cooperate with the Sun. Then, we no longer would be simple speaking machines as we are currently, since we would transform ourselves into real humans, into kings and queens of creation.

Therefore, to state that this humanity is made up by humans is an exaggeration. I understand that the human being is the lord, the king, the queen of creation. The Bible states that the human was made to govern the animal and plant species, to govern the ocean, the air, and the fire. Therefore, if one is not a king, if one is not a queen of creation, then one is not an authentic human.

Who of you can govern the elements? Who of you can provoke a storm? Who of you is able to appease a fire? Who of you is able to activate the volcanoes of the Earth, or to make the earth to tremble, to produce an earthquake or to calm it? If we are not lords of creation, then we are not human, because in the Bible it is written that the human is the king of creation. Therefore, are we kings or not? If we are victims of circumstances, if an earthquake kills thousands of people, as is happening in the whole world, then what do you think? Are we victims of circumstances? Where are the human beings? If the elements can destroy us in the same manner as we destroy an anthill with our foot, then where are the qualities of the true human that everybody states we have?

Indeed, even if we presume we are humans, we are in reality nothing more than simple intellectual animals who are sentenced to live the sadness of life. Yet, the seed of the true human exists within our glands. Yes, such a seed can transform us into solar humans. This seed can germinate within us if we cooperate with the Sun and its solar ideas. The Sun has created this root race not only to be useful to the economy of Nature, but also with the clear intention of attaining a harvest of solar humans.

In the times of Abraham the prophet, the Sun acquired a beautiful harvest of solar humans. During the first eight centuries of Christianity, another small harvest was reaped. In the Middle Ages, a few more. Presently, the Sun is perform- ing the last effort; it has been working its last effort. Because the perverse human- ity of this present century has become an enemy of the solar ideas, this humanity is terribly materialistic, mechanical and one hundred percent lunar. This is why the Sun is now making a last effort; it is try- ing to get a small harvest of solar humans. Later, once the harvest is ready, the Sun will destroy this root race because it is no longer useful for its experiment.

What is this race useful for? There is already no reason for the existence of this race. It is not useful for the solar experiment. This humanity is made up of people that have no interest in the solar ideas. This root race thinks only of their bank accounts, of new cars, of the actors and actresses in Hollywood. These are people who only want passionate, sexual pleasures, drugs, etc.

Obviously, this humanity is not useful for the solar experiment. People like this have to be destroyed, and this is what the Sun is going to do. The Sun will destroy these people and will create a new root race in new continents that will emerge from the bottom of the ocean.

Very soon, the present continents will be at the bottom of the oceans. The palaces of governments, the municipal houses, the rich mansions will be lairs for seals and fish. This is the reality! New lands will emerge from the oceans in which, obviously, there will be new people, a special, different race that could be useful to the solar experiment.

This is the reality. I am stating this in anguishing times, in times where the people do not believe in the end of the world, in times in which the people say, "Let us eat and drink, because tomorrow we will die," in times in which people are only concerned about their bank accounts, fashion, gossip, drugs, or lewdness.

Therefore, I am stating all of this with the intention of inviting you to reflect...

Is it possible for the solar seed to germinate? Yes, as the butterfly is born inside of the chrysalis; likewise, the seed exists in order to make the true human to be born inside of us. But, first of all, it is necessary to have the suitability of being a human. If the suitability of being a human does not exist, the human cannot be born inside of us.

The seed exists, yet it can be lost, and this is normal since this seed is very difficult to germinate. We need to develop this seed. We can do it if we cooperate with the Sun.

So, this present humanity has three percent awakened consciousness and ninety-seven percent of their consciousness asleep. That is why it is in such a critical state.

People in general want to see, hear, touch or experience the great realities of the superior worlds, namely to remember their past reincarnations, to talk with the angels, etc. However, unfortunately, as we have already stated, people have three percent awakened consciousness and ninety seven percent of their consciousness asleep.

Therefore, whosoever wants to experience the great realities of the interior worlds, such as the astral world, the mental world, the spiritual world, etc., has to become a solar human with an awakened consciousness. To attain this, one has to have the resolution of psychologically dying from moment to moment. This is indispensable.

First of all, it is necessary to know that we have a pluralized "I" or ego within each one of us. Such an "I" is Seth from Egyptian mythology, who is a conjunction of "red devils" as it was stated by the ancient priests of the land of the Pharaohs.

Thus, these submerged entities, which personify the ego or Seth, as we already stated, are the semblance of our own particular defects.

Our consciousness is bottled up, trapped, asleep within each one of those entities. Therefore, our consciousness acts in accordance with its conditioning; that is to say, it definitively advances along the path of error. This is because the nature of our consciousness is unfortunately egoic.

If we want to awaken in order to see, hear, touch or experience everything from the superior dimensions, such as to converse with the solar humans or masters of the White Fraternity,[7] then it is necessary to totally destroy Seth, the ego, the red devils, the psychological "I's."

Only through this annihilation can the consciousness become emancipated, liberated, and radically awakened.

When the consciousness awakens, then we can see the secret path. When the consciousness awakens, we can place ourselves in contact with the divine solar humanity who live in the Jinn lands.[8] When the consciousness awakens, we can then remember our past reincarnations or visit other inhabited planets or talk face to face with the solar angels of the mahamanvantara,[9] etc.

Therefore, dear reader, only with the awakened consciousness can we have direct knowledge. Hence, while we do not attain direct knowledge, we are nothing other than intellectual ignoramuses who repeat like parrots what others say. That is all.

We need to experience with our consciousness all that we study. We need to

---

7   See glossary.
8   The fourth dimension, also called "Eden."
9   Sanskrit, "great cosmic day."

drink directly from the fountain of the solar wisdom. I, Samael Aun Weor, can teach
you and am teaching you what I know,
what I experienced, what I have lived, not
only in this present reincarnation, but
also in my past reincarnations. Moreover,
I can talk with you in a blunt and sincere
way about events of past cosmic days,
because I was active in past cosmic days.
Therefore, I can give testimony of what
I directly experienced, of what I saw and
heard. This is not a crime.

Therefore, allow me to sincerely tell
you that in order to awaken the consciousness and to become a solar human,
one needs tremendous esoteric discipline.

So, dear reader, in order to be a psychologically awakened individual, an illumi-
nated one, a solar being, it is indispensable to dissolve the ego.

To comprehend each one of our defects
is not enough. It is necessary to know how
to eliminate them.

Krishnamurti talks to us about comprehension. He is right because it is
necessary to comprehend each one of our
errors. If for instance one wants to eliminate the defect of anger, then one needs to
comprehend that particular "I." We need

to perform the meditation, the reflection on this particular anger, in order to know its most secret impulses. Since there are many sources of anger, one can be angry for this or that reason. For instance, one can be angry because somebody hurt our self-esteem or because of jealousy or because of an emotional frustration or because of a reaction when listening to a certain unpleasant word. Anger has too many faces.

Once one has comprehended the secret impulse of any explosion of anger in any given moment, then one has to be assisted by a superior force. This superior force is within each one of us. It is the serpentine solar fire who can activate our solar power that is enclosed, as is stated by the Hindus, within the Muladhara chakra, which is situated in the coccyx. I am emphatically referring to Devi Kundalini,[10] the serpentine solar fire, who can activate our solar powers.

One needs to work with her, with the Kundalini. Yes, one needs to be assisted by her; one needs to ask her, to beg her,

---

10 The serpent of brass of Moses, the Shekinah of Kabbalah, the fire of Pentecost, the serpent of Athena, etc. See glossary.

to beseech her to eliminate that "I" of anger, that one that was comprehended in depth, that one that was studied through deepest meditation and reflection.

The procedure is the same for any psychological defect, trauma etc. For it is not enough to comprehend the secret impulses of an explosion of jealousy or the origin of certain hatred. One needs to go further beyond and to be assisted by a superior power. This is the Kundalini.

The mind is not capable of eliminating a defect. The mind can label it with many names, it can move the defect from one level into another; yet, it cannot disintegrate it, it cannot reduce it into dust.

Therefore, if we want to reduce this or that defect which is personified in this or that "I" into dust, then besides comprehension, one needs elimination. In order to eliminate, one needs to be assisted by Devi Kundalini.

Devi Kundalini is the serpentine solar fire who can activate our solar powers. She is that fiery serpent or serpent of brass who healed the Israelites in the wilderness.

"Nonetheless, frustrated people, tired of suffering,
want to change, to turn the page of their history…"

Chapter 1

The Level of Being

Who are we? Where do we come from? Where are we going? What are we living for? Why are we living?

Unquestionably, the wretched "intellectual animal," mistakenly called a human being, not only ignores, but furthermore ignores that he ignores.

The worst of it is the strange and difficult situation in which we find ourselves; we ignore the secret of all our tragedies, yet we are convinced that we know it all.

Just send a "rational mammal" to the middle of the Sahara desert, one of those who claims to be influential in life; leave him there, far away from any oasis, and observe from an airplane what occurs. Facts will speak for themselves: the "intellectual humanoid," though he boasts that he is powerful and believes he is a real human being, turns out to be frightfully weak.

The "rational animal" is one hundred percent stupid. He thinks the best of himself. He thinks he can develop his potential via kindergarten, good manners, elementary and secondary schools, diplomas, universities, the prestige of daddy, etc.

Unfortunately, in spite of so much education, good manners, titles, and money, we know very well that any stomachache saddens us, and that deep down we continue being unhappy and miserable.

It is enough to read universal history to find out that we are still the same barbarians of the past, and instead of improving, we have become worse.

This present century with its magnificence, wars, prostitution, world-wide sodomy, sexual degeneration, drugs, alcohol, exorbitant cruelty, extreme perversion, monstrosity, etc., is the mirror in which we must see ourselves; there is not a good enough reason to boast of having reached a superior stage of development.

To think that time means progress is absurd; unfortunately, the "learned ignoramuses" continue to be bottled up in the "dogma of evolution..."

In all the somber pages of "dark history" we find the same atrocious cruelties, ambitions, wars, etc. Nevertheless, our "super-civilized" contemporaries are still convinced that what we hear about war is secondary, a fleeting accident that has nothing to do with their so-boasted "modern civilization."

Indeed, what is important is the way of being of each person. Some subjects will be drunkards; others will be abstemious, some honest and others shameless; there is everything in life.

The populace is the sum of all individuals. The populace is what the individual is; it is the government, etc... The populace, then, is the extension of the individual; it is impossible to change people and populace if the individual does not change himself.

Nobody can deny the fact that there are different social levels. There are churchgoing people, people in brothels, farmers, businessmen, etc. In a like manner, there are different Levels of Being. Whatever we are internally—munificent or mean, generous or miserly, violent or peaceful, chaste or lustful—attracts the various circumstances of life.

The lustful person will always attract scenes, dramas and even lascivious tragedies in which he will become involved.

A drunkard will always attract drunkards and will always be seen in bars or taverns; this is obvious...

What will the usurer attract? The selfish one? How many problems? Jail? Misfortunes?

Nonetheless, frustrated people, tired of suffering, want to change, to turn the page of their history...

Wretched people! They want to change and they do not know how; they do not know the methods; they are stuck in a blind alley.

What happened to them yesterday happens to them today, and will happen to them again tomorrow; they always repeat the same errors and not even cannon shots will make them learn the lessons of life.

All things repeat themselves in their life; they say the same things, do the same things and complain about the same things.

This boring repetition of dramas, comedies, and tragedies will continue as long as we carry in our interior all the undesirable elements of anger, covetousness, lust, envy, pride, laziness, gluttony, etc.

What is our moral level? Or better said, what is our Level of Being?

The repetition of all our miseries, scenes, misfortunes, and mishaps will last as long as the Level of our Being does not radically change.

All things, all circumstances that occur outside ourselves on the stage of this world, are exclusively the reflection of what we carry within.

With good reason then, we can solemnly declare that the "exterior is the reflection of the interior."

When someone changes internally—and if that change is radical—then circumstances, life, and the external also change.

Not long ago, since 1974, I have been observing a group of people who invaded a private estate ground. Here in Mexico such people receive the strange name of "parachutists."

They are neighbors from the rural colony of Churubusco; they are very close to my home and that is why I have been able to study them closely.

To be poor will certainly never be a crime; however, their serious problem does not lie in poverty but rather in their Level of Being.

They fight amongst themselves daily, get drunk, insult each other, become the murderers of their own companions who share their misfortunes, and live in filthy huts where hatred reigns instead of love.

Many times I have pondered on the fact that if any one of them would eliminate from his interior hatred, anger, lust, slander, drunkenness, cruelty, egoism, calumny, envy, conceit, pride, etc., he would please other people, and by the simple law of psychological affinities, he would associate with more refined and spiritual people. These new relationships would definitely bring about an economical and social change. This would be the way out of the "pigsty," the "filthy sewer," for this individual...

Therefore, if we really want a radical change, the first thing we must understand is that each one of us (whether black or white, yellow or brunette, ignorant or erudite, etc.), is at one "Level of Being" or another.

What is our Level of Being? Have you ever reflected upon this? It would be impossible to pass into another level if we ignore the level in which we presently are.

Chapter 2

The Marvelous Ladder

We must long for a real change; we must get out of this boring routine, out of this purely mechanical and wearied life.

What we must first clearly understand is that each one of us is at one Level of Being or another.

The Level of Being of the drunkard is different from that of the abstemious, and the Level of Being of the prostitute is different from that of the virgin. What we are stating here is indisputable, irrefutable.

Advancing on the theme of this chapter, it is not irrelevant if we imagine the numerous rungs of a ladder which extends itself upwards, vertically.

Unquestionably, we find ourselves on any one of these rungs. On the lower rungs will be people worse than us, and on the higher rungs persons better than us will be found.

On this extraordinary vertical, on this "marvelous ladder," it is clear that we can find all the Levels of Being.

Each person is different; this is something that no one can dispute.

Undoubtedly, we are not talking about pretty or ugly faces, nor is it a question of age. There are young and old people, old persons about to die as well as newborns.

The subject matter of time and of years, that matter of being born, of maturing, developing, marrying, reproducing and aging is exclusively of the horizontal.

On the "marvelous ladder," on the vertical, the concept of time does not fit in. On the rungs of such a scale we can only find Levels of Being.

The mechanical hope of people serves no purpose. They think that with time things will get better. Our grandfather and great grandfathers thought that way; however, facts have arrived to precisely demonstrate the opposite of this.

What counts is the Level of Being, and this is vertical. We are on a rung, but we can climb to another rung.

The "marvelous ladder" of which we are talking and which concerns the different Levels of Being certainly has nothing to do with linear time.

A higher Level of Being is directly above us from moment to moment. It is not in any remote horizontal future but here and now within our very selves, on the vertical.

It is clear, and anyone can understand, that the two lines, horizontal and vertical, intersect from moment to moment in our psychological interior and form a cross.

The personality develops and unfolds on the horizontal line of life. The personality is born and dies with its linear time; it is mortal. There is no "tomorrow" for the personality of the dead person. The personality is not the Being.[1]

The Levels of Being are not of time. Since the Being himself is not of time, He has nothing to do with the horizontal line. He is found within ourselves, now, on the vertical.

It would be absurd, obviously, to look for our own Being outside of ourselves. Therefore, it is not irrelevant to establish the following as a corollary: titles, ranks, promotions, etc. in the external physical world cannot in any way originate authentic exaltation, re-evaluation of the Being, or a move to a higher rung in the Levels of Being.

---

1   Divinity within us.

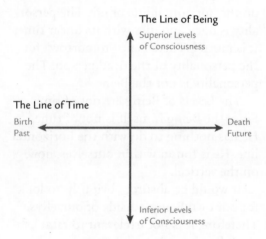

The Line of Being

Superior Levels
of Consciousness

The Line of Time

Birth
Past

Death
Future

Inferior Levels
of Consciousness

Chapter 3

Psychological Rebellion

It is not irrelevant to remind our readers that a mathematical point exists within us. Unquestionably, that point is not found in the past or in the future. Whosoever wants to discover that mysterious point must look for it here and now within oneself at this exact moment, not a second earlier, not a second later.

The two horizontal and vertical lines of the Holy Cross intersect at this point.

Thus, we find ourselves from moment to moment before two paths: the horizontal and the vertical.

It is apparent that the horizontal path is too base; it is traveled by my buddy and everybody, by those who are juvenile and those who are senile.

It is evident that the vertical is different; it is the path of intelligent rebels, of revolutionaries.

When one remembers oneself and works upon oneself, when one does not become identified with all the problems and sorrows of life, it is a fact that one is traveling along the vertical path.

Certainly, it is never an easy task to eliminate negative emotions, to lose all identification with our trend of life, with all types of problems, with business, debts, loan payments, mortgages, telephone, water and power payments, etc.

The unemployed ones, those who have lost their position or job for one reason or another, evidently suffer because of lack of money and for them to forget their situation and not worry or identify themselves with their own problem becomes tremendously difficult.

Those who suffer and those who cry, those who have been victims of some betrayal or injustice, victims of ingratitude, calumny, fraud, really do forget themselves; they forget their Inner Being; they identify themselves totally with their moral tragedy.

The work on oneself is the fundamental characteristic of the vertical path.

Nobody treads upon the path of the great rebellion if he never works on himself.

The work to which we are referring is of a psychological nature. This work deals with a certain transformation of the moment in which we find ourselves.

We need to learn to live from moment to moment.

For example, a person who is desperate about some sentimental, economical or political problems has obviously forgotten his inner Self.

If such a person would stop for a moment, observe the situation, try to remember his inner Self and then try to understand the reason for this attitude...

If he would reflect a little and think that everything passes away, that life is fleeting, illusory, and that death reduces all the vanities of the world to ashes...

If he would understand that his problem in reality is nothing more than a worthless flame and soon dies, he would suddenly see with great surprise that everything has changed.

It is possible to transform mechanical reactions through logical confrontation and the intimate auto-reflection of the Being.

It is evident that people react mechanically when faced with the diverse circumstances of life.

Wretched people, they usually become the victims. When flattered, they smile, when humiliated, they suffer. They insult if insulted, they hurt if they are hurt; they are never free; their fellowmen have the power to drive them from happiness to sadness, from hope to despair.

Each of these persons traveling along the horizontal path is similar to a musical instrument on which each of his fellowmen can play the tune he wishes.

Whosoever learns how to transform mechanical reactions is in fact entering onto the vertical path.

This represents a fundamental change in the "Level of Being," an extraordinary result of the "psychological rebellion."

Chapter 4

The Essence

What makes every newborn child beautiful and adorable is its Essence.[2] The Essence constitutes its true reality.

In all creatures, the normal growth of the Essence is certainly scanty, insufficient.

The human body grows and develops in accordance with the biological laws of the species; however, such possibilities in themselves are extremely limited for the Essence.

---

2   From the Chinese 體 ti, which literally means "substance, body" and is often translated as "essence," to indicate that which is always there throughout transformations. In gnosis, the term essence refers to our consciousness, which remains fundamentally the same, in spite of the many transformations it suffers, especially life, death, and being trapped in psychological defects. A common example given in Buddhism is a glass of water: even if filled with dirt and impurities, the water is still there. However, one would not want to drink it that way. Just so with the Essence (the consciousness): our Essence is trapped in impurities; to use it properly, it must be cleaned first. See glossary for more information.

INSIDE OF THE GREAT SPIRITUAL HEROES, PERSEUS (THE SOUL) KILLS
MEDUSA (THE EGO, THE "FIERY SERPENTS" THAT BIT THE ISRAELITES).

Unquestionably, without help, the Essence can only grow to a small degree.

Speaking frankly and bluntly, we will say that the spontaneous and natural growth of the Essence is only possible during the first three, four and five years of life; in other words, during the first phase of life.

People think that the growth and development of the Essence always occurs in a continuous way, according to the mechanics of evolution, but universal Gnosticism teaches clearly that this does not occur in such a manner.

Something very special must happen, something new must be fulfilled so that the Essence may grow more.

I want to emphatically refer to the work upon oneself. The development of the Essence is only possible on the basis of conscious works and voluntary sufferings.

It is necessary to understand that this work does not refer to professional matters such as banking, carpentry, masonry, railroad repairs, or office matters.

This work is for any person who has developed his personality; it concerns something psychological.

We all know that we have within ourselves that which is called ego, I, me,
myself.

Unfortunately, the Essence is completely imprisoned, absorbed inside the
ego, and this is lamentable.

To dissolve the psychological "I," to
disintegrate its undesirable elements, is
something unavoidable and non-excludable. This is the meaning of working
upon oneself.

We would never be able to liberate the
Essence without previously disintegrating
the psychological "I."

Religion, the Buddha, Wisdom, the
particles in pain of our Father who is
in heaven, and all the information we
need for the realization of our Innermost
Self, of our Inner Being, are within the
Essence.

No one would be able to annihilate
the psychological "I" without previously
eliminating the inhuman elements that
we carry within ourselves.

We need to reduce to ashes the monstrous cruelty of this day and age: envy
which has unfortunately become the
secret trigger of action, the unbearable
covetousness that has made life so bitter,

the disgusting slander, the calumny which gives rise to so many tragedies, the drunken revelries, the filthy lust that smells so hideously, etc.

Accordingly, as all these abominations are being reduced to cosmic dust, the Essence, besides becoming emancipated, will harmoniously grow and develop.

Unquestionably, the Essence shines within ourselves when our psychological "I" has died.

The liberated Essence confers upon us inner beauty. Perfect happiness and true love emanate from such a beauty.

The Essence possesses multiple senses of perfection and extraordinary natural powers.

When we die within ourselves, when we dissolve the psychological "I," we can then enjoy the precious senses and powers of the Essence.

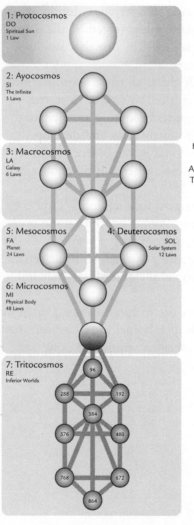

1: Protocosmos
DO
Spiritual Sun
1 Law

2: Ayocosmos
SI
The Infinite
3 Laws

3: Macrocosmos
LA
Galaxy
6 Laws

5: Mesocosmos
FA
Planet
24 Laws

4: Deuterocosmos
SOL
Solar System
12 Laws

6: Microcosmos
MI
Physical Body
48 Laws

7: Tritocosmos
RE
Inferior Worlds

96
288   192
384
576   480
768   672
864

HOW THE LIGHT
FLOWS FROM
ABOVE TO BELOW.
THE TREE OF LIFE
(KABBALAH)

Chapter 5

To Accuse Oneself

The Essence that each one of us carries in our interior comes from above, from Heaven, from the stars...

Unquestionably, the marvelous Essence emanates from the note La (the Milky Way, the galaxy we live in).

The precious Essence passes through the note Sol (the Sun), and then passes through the note Fa (the planetary zone), then enters this world and enters our interior.

Our parents created the appropriate body for the reception of this Essence that emanates from the stars...

We return victoriously into the profound bosom of "Urania" by working intensely upon ourselves and sacrificing ourselves for our fellowmen.

We are living in this world for some reason, for something, for some special factor...

Obviously, there is much in us that we must see, study and comprehend, if indeed to know something about ourselves, about our own life is what we long for...

Tragic is the existence of the one who dies without having known the purpose of his life...

Each one of us must discover for himself the purpose of his own life, to discover what is that which keeps him prisoner within the prison of pain...

Clearly, there is something within us that makes our life bitter, and this is what we need to firmly struggle against...

It is not required that we continue in disgrace; therefore, it is urgent that we reduce to cosmic dust what makes us so weak and miserable.

It is useless for us to be conceited about ranks, honors, diplomas, money, vain subjective rationalism, aforementioned virtues, etc.

We must never forget that hypocrisy and the silly vanities of our false personality make us dull, rancid, retarded, reactionary, and incapable of seeing the new.

Death has many meanings, both positive and negative. Let us consider the magnificent observation of the great Kabir Jesus the Christ, "Let the dead bury their dead." Many people, although alive, are in fact dead to all possible work upon themselves and therefore to any inner transformation.

They are people imprisoned in their dogmas and beliefs, people petrified in memories of many yesterdays, individuals full of ancestral prejudices, persons who are the slave of what others might say, horribly lukewarm, indifferent and sometimes "know it all ignoramuses" who are convinced that they are right because that is what they were told, etc.

Those people do not want to understand that this world is a "psychological gymnasium" through which it would be possible to annihilate that secret ugliness that we all carry within.

If those wretched people comprehended the lamentable state in which they dwell, they would tremble with horror...

Nonetheless, such people think the best of themselves. They boast of their virtues. They feel they are perfect, generous, helpful, noble, charitable, intelligent, responsible, etc.

Practical life as a school is formidable, but to take it as a goal in itself is manifestly an absurdity.

Those who take life in itself, such as it is daily lived, have not comprehended the necessity of working upon themselves in order to achieve a "radical transformation."

Unfortunately, people live mechanically and have never heard anything about the inner work...

Change is necessary but people do not know how to change. They suffer greatly, however they do not even know why they suffer.

Money is not everything. Usually, the life of many wealthy people is truly tragic.

Chapter 6
Life

In the field of practical life, we discover astonishing contrasts. Wealthy people with a magnificent residence and with many friends sometimes suffer terribly.

Humble proletarians of picks and shovels or middle class people often live in complete happiness.

Many multi-millionaires suffer from sexual impotence and rich matrons cry bitterly due to their husbands' infidelities...

In this day and age, the rich people of the earth look like vultures in golden cages. They cannot live without bodyguards.

Statesmen drag chains; they are never free; wherever they go they are surrounded by people armed to the teeth...

Let us study this situation more in detail. We need to know what life is. Everyone is free to think as he likes...

Regardless of whatever people say, indeed, nobody knows anything. Life is a problem that no one understands...

When people want to freely tell us the story of their life, they quote events, names and surnames, dates, etc. and feel satisfaction when telling their stories...

Those wretched people ignore that their stories are incomplete because events, names and dates are merely the outer aspect of the movie; the inner aspect is missing...

It is urgent to know "states of consciousness." Each event is complemented with this or that psychological state.

The states are internal and the events are external. So, external events are not everything.

Let it be understood that internal states are good or bad disposition, preoccupation, depression, superstition, fear, suspicion, mercy, self-commiseration, overestimation of oneself, states of one's sentiments of happiness, states of pleasure, etc.

Unquestionably, internal states can correspond exactly to external events, they can be originated by the latter, or they may not have any relationship with them whatsoever.

In every case, states and events are different. Events do not always correspond exactly to compatible states.

A pleasant event could be unrelated with its internal state.

An unpleasant event could be unrelated with its internal state.

When long awaited for events finally take place, we often feel that something is missing...

Certainly, the corresponding internal state which should have been combined with the external event was missing...

Many times an unexpected event comes to be the one that has provided us with the best moments.

THE PILGRIM BY WILLIAM BLAKE

Chapter 7
The Internal State

To correctly combine internal states with external events is to know how to live intelligently...

Any event intelligently lived demands its corresponding specific internal state...

Nonetheless, when people review their lives, unfortunately, they only think that their life is exclusively constituted by external events...

Wretched people! They think that if this or that event had never happened to them, their lives would have been better...

They think that fortune came to meet them, yet they lost the opportunity to be happy...

They lament what they lost, they weep regarding what they despised; they moan when remembering their old errors and calamities...

People do not want to realize that to vegetate is not to live and that the capacity to consciously exist depends exclusively on the quality of the interior states of the Soul...

Certainly, it does not matter how beautiful the external events of life might be; if we are not in the appropriate internal state in those moments, the best moments can seem monotonous, tiresome or simply boring to us...

Someone anxiously awaits the wedding banquet as a great event. Nevertheless, it could happen that he could be so preoccupied in that precise moment that he really would not enjoy it. Thus, that party would become for him as dry and cold as protocol.

Experience has taught us that not all persons who attend a banquet or a party really enjoy themselves.

A bored person is always present at the best of parties and the most delightful musical compositions make some people happy and make others weep.

Those who know how to consciously combine the external event with the appropriate interior state are very rare.

It is unfortunate that people do not know how to consciously live; they weep when they should laugh and laugh when they should weep.

Control is different; the sage can be happy but never filled with an insane frenzy, sad but never desperate and discouraged, calm in the middle of violence, abstinent in the orgy, chaste when amidst lust, etc.

Melancholic and pessimistic persons think the worst of life and frankly they do not want to live.

Everyday we see people that are not only unhappy, but moreover, what is even worse, they make other people's lives miserable.

Such people will not change, even if they would live daily from party to party, for they carry the psychological disease within them... Such persons possess internal states that are definitely perverse...

Nevertheless, these people classify themselves as just, saintly, virtuous, noble, helpful, martyrs, etc.

They are people who esteem themselves to the extreme; people who love themselves too much...

They are individuals who pity themselves too much and seek a way out to evade their own responsibilities...

Persons like that are accustomed to inferior emotions and it is obvious that due to such a motive, they daily create infra-human psychic elements.

Disgraceful events like the setbacks of fortune, misery, debts, problems, etc. are the exclusive property of those persons who do not know how to live...

Anyone can acquire a rich intellectual culture; yet, few are the persons who have learned how to live in an upright manner...

When one wants to separate external events from the internal states of consciousness, one demonstrates concretely his incapacity of existing in a dignified manner.

Those who learn how to consciously combine external events with internal states march on the path of success.

Chapter 8

Erroneous States

Unquestionably, while in rigorous observation of the "myself," a complete logical differentiation between the exterior events of practical life and the interior states of the consciousness is always something unavoidable and non-excludable.

We urgently need to know where we are located relative to the interior state of consciousness, as well as to the specific nature of the exterior event that is happening to us in a given moment.

Life in itself is a series of events that process themselves through time and space. Someone said, "Life is a chain of woes that humans carry entangled in their souls."

Everyone is free to think as he wishes. I believe that disenchantment and bitterness always proceed the ephemeral pleasures of a fleeting moment.

Each event has its special characteristic flavor. The interior states also are of a distinct type. This is incontrovertible, irrefutable.

Indeed, the interior work upon oneself emphatically refers to the diverse psychological states of the consciousness.

No one can deny that in our interior we carry many errors and that erroneous states also exist.

If indeed we want to change, we need with maximum and unavoidable urgency to radically modify those erroneous states of our consciousness.

The absolute modification of the erroneous states originates complete transformations in the field of practical life.

Obviously, when one seriously works on the erroneous states, then the unpleasant events of life can no longer hurt so easily.

We are stating something that can only be comprehended by living it, when indeed one experiences it precisely in the field of actions.

Whosoever does not work on himself is always a victim of circumstances; he is like a miserable log on the boisterous waters of the ocean.

Events incessantly change in their multiple combinations. They come one after another in waves; they are influences...

Indeed, there are good and bad events. Some events will be better or worse than others.

Certainly, to modify certain events, to alter results, to modify situations, etc., is possible amidst the number of possibilities.

However, there are some factual situations which truly cannot be altered.

These cases must be consciously accepted, even when some become dangerous and even painful...

Unquestionably, such a grief disappears when we do not identify ourselves with the problem that has arisen...

We must consider life as a successive series of interior states. The authentic history of our life in particular is formed by these states...

When reviewing the totality of our own existence, we can then verify for ourselves in a direct manner that many unpleasant situations were possible thanks to wrong interior states...

Although Alexander the Great was always temperate by nature, he gave in, due to pride, to the excesses which produced his death...

Francis I died due to a dirty and abominable adultery, which is still well remembered in history...

When Marat was assassinated by a perverse nun, he was dying of arrogance and envy, he believed himself to be absolutely just...

Unquestionably, the ladies of the "Parc des Cerfs" totally exhausted the vitality of the horrible fornicator Louis XV.

Due to jealousy, Othello became an assassin.

Many are the people who die of ambition, anger or jealousy; this is well known by psychologists...

When our will irrevocably fixes itself on an absurd tendency, we become candidates for the pantheon or cemetery...

Therefore, jails are filled with sincerely mistaken people.

Chapter 9
Personal Events

When dealing with the discovery of
wrong psychological states, a complete
intimate self-observation of the "myself"
is unavoidable.

Unquestionably, wrong internal states
can be corrected with correct procedures.

Since our internal life is the magnet
which attracts external events, we need
with a maximum and unavoidable urgency to eliminate erroneous psychological
states from our psyche.

The correction of mistaken psychological states is indispensable when one wants
to fundamentally alter the nature of certain undesirable events.

The alteration of our relation with
certain events is possible if we eliminate
certain absurd psychological states from
our interior.

Destructive external situations could
become inoffensive and even constructive by intelligently correcting erroneous
internal states.

When one purifies oneself internally, one can then change the nature of unpleasant events that happen to us.

Whosoever never corrects absurd psychological states, believing himself to be very strong, becomes a victim of circumstances.

When one wishes to change the course of an unhappy existence, it is then vital to establish an order within one's disorderly internal house.

People complain about everything. They suffer, cry, protest. They would like to change their life, to come out of the misfortune they are having; yet unfortunately, they do not work upon themselves.

People do not want to realize that their internal life attracts external circumstances. Therefore, if the external circumstances are painful, it is because of their absurd internal states.

The external is merely the reflection of the internal. Therefore, whosoever changes internally originates a new order of things.

The external events are never as important as the way one reacts when facing them.

Did you remain serene before the offender? Did you gladly receive the unpleasant manifestations of your fellow-men?

How did you react to the infidelity of your beloved one? Did you let yourself be carried away by the poison of jealousy? Did you kill? Are you in prison?

Hospitals, cemeteries or pantheons, and prisons are filled with sincerely mistaken ones who reacted in an absurd manner when faced with external events.

The best weapon that a human being can use in life is a correct psychological state.

One can disarm beasts and unmask traitors by means of appropriate internal states.

Wrong internal states convert us into defenseless victims of human perversity.

You must learn to face the most unpleasant events of practical life with an appropriate internal uprightness...

You must not become identified with any event. Remember that everything passes away. You must learn to look at life like a movie; thus, you shall receive the benefits...

You must not forget that if you do
not eliminate mistaken internal states
from your psyche, then events of no value
could bring you disgrace.

Unquestionably, each external event
needs its appropriate fare, that is, its precise psychological state.

Chapter 10

The Different "I's"

Indeed, the rational mammal mistakenly called the human being does not possess a defined individuality.

Unquestionably, this lack of psychological unity in the humanoid is the cause of so many difficulties and bitterness.

The physical body is a complete unit and works as an organic whole unless it is ill.

However, the internal life of the humanoid is in no way a psychological unit.

The most critical aspect of all of this, in spite of what the diverse pseudo-esoteric and pseudo-occultist schools might say, is the lack of psychological organization in the intimate depths of each person.

Certainly in those conditions, an accordant work, as a complete harmonious unit in the internal life of people, does not exist.

The humanoid, in regards to his internal state, is a psychological multiplicity, a sum of "I's."

The learned ignoramuses of this tenebrous era pay homage to the "I;" they deify it; they place it on altars; they name it alter-ego, superior "I," divine "I," etc.

The "know-it-alls" of this dark age in which we live do not want to realize that the superior "I" or the inferior "I" are two sections of the same pluralized ego...

Indeed, the humanoid does not have a permanent "I," but instead he has a multitude of different infra-human and absurd "I's."

The wretched intellectual animal mistakenly called a human being is similar to a house in disorder where instead of one lord, there are many servants who always want to command and to perform their own whims.

The greatest error of cheap pseudo-esotericism and pseudo-occultism is to assume that others possess or that one has a permanent and immutable "I," without a beginning and an end...

If for at least one instant those who think in the way previously described were to awaken consciousness, they would then clearly see for themselves that the rational humanoid is never the same "one" through a long period of time...

Thus, from a psychological point of view, the intellectual mammal is continuously changing...

To think that a person named Louis is always Louis is like a joke made in very bad taste...

That subject called Louis has other "I's," other "egos" in himself, who, in different moments, express themselves through his personality. Therefore, even if Louis does not like covetousness, another "I" within him, let's call him Peter, likes covetousness, and so on...

No person is the same in a continuous manner. Indeed, one does not have to be a sage in order to fully realize the innumerable changes and contradictions of each individual...

Therefore, to assume that someone possesses a permanent and immutable "I" is equivalent to committing an abuse against our fellowmen and against oneself...

Thus, many people, many "I's," live inside each person. Any awakened or conscious person can, in a direct way, verify this by himself...

The Temptation of St. Anthony by the Many I's

Chapter 11

The Beloved Ego

Since superior and inferior are two portions of the same thing, it is not irrelevant to state the following corollary: superior "I" and inferior "I" are two aspects of the same tenebrous and pluralized ego.

The so-called divine "I" or superior "I," alter-ego or anything of the sort, is certainly a trick of the "myself," a form of self-deceit.

When the "I" wants to continue here and in the beyond, it deceives itself with the false concept of being a divine and immortal "I."

None of us has a true "I" that is permanent, immutable, eternal, ineffable, etc.

Indeed, none of us has a true and authentic unity of Being. Unfortunately, we do not even possess legitimate individuality.

Although the ego continues beyond the sepulcher, it has, nonetheless, a beginning and an end.

The ego, the "I," is never something individual, unitary, a total unity.
Obviously, the "I" is "I's."

In Asian Tibet, the "I's" are called
psychic aggregates, or simply positive or
negative values.

If we think of each "I" as a different
person, we can then emphatically state
the following, "Within each person living
in the world, there are many people."

Unquestionably, many different persons live inside each one of us, some of
them are better than others, and others
are worse...

Each one of these "I's," each one of
these persons, struggles for supremacy.

As often as possible, each one of these
"I's" wants to be exclusive. Each one
wants to control the intellectual brain or
the emotional and motor centers until
another substitutes it...

The Doctrine of the Many "I's" was
taught in Asian Tibet by the true clairvoy-
ants, by the true enlightened ones...

Each of our defects is personified by
one "I" or another. Since we have thousands and even millions of defects, it is
obvious that many people live within our
interior.

In psychological matters, we have been able to clearly verify that paranoid subjects, self-worshippers and mythomaniacs would never abandon the cult to their beloved ego for anything in the world.

Unquestionably, such people mortally hate the Doctrine of the Many "I's."

Indeed, when one wants to know oneself, one must observe himself and try to know the different "I's" which abound inside the personality.

If any one of our readers does not yet comprehend the Doctrine of the Many "I's," it is due exclusively to the lack of practice in the field of self-observation.

As one practices inner self-observation, one discovers for oneself many people, many "I's," who live inside our own personality.

Those who deny the Doctrine of the Many "I's," those who adore a divine "I," have undoubtedly never observed themselves seriously.

Pointing at them, this time in a Socratic style, we state that those people not only ignore, but more over, they ignore that they ignore.

Certainly, we can never know ourselves without serious and profound self-observation.

As long as any person continues considering himself as only one, it is clear that any internal change would be something more than impossible.

Chapter 12
Radical Change

As long as a person persists in the error of believing himself to be one unique individual, it is evident that radical change would be more than impossible.

The very fact that the esoteric work begins with the rigorous observation of oneself is indicating to us a multiplicity of psychological factors, "I's" or undesirable elements that need to be urgently extirpated, eradicated from our interior.

Unquestionably, it would not be possible in any way to eliminate unknown errors. It is urgent to previously observe that which we want to separate from our psyche.

This type of work is not external but internal, and those who think that any manual of manners or external and superficial system of ethics can take them to success are, in fact, totally mistaken.

The concrete and definite fact that the internal work begins with attention, which is concentrated in the full observation of oneself, is more than enough reason to demonstrate that this demands a very particular and personal effort from each one of us.

Speaking frankly and bluntly, we emphatically affirm the following: no human being could do this work for us.

No change whatsoever is possible within our psyche without the direct observation of the whole sum of subjective factors that we carry within.

When the multiplicity of our errors is accepted as something factual, yet one discards the necessity of study and direct observation of the errors, it is an evasion or escape, an escape from oneself, a form of self-deceit.

Indeed, it is only by applying a rigorous effort and a judicious observation of the myself, without evasions of any type, that we will be able to verify that we are not "one" but "many."

To admit to the plurality of the "I" and to experience it through rigorous observation are two different aspects.

Someone could admit to the Doctrine of the Many "I's," without ever having experienced it. The latter is possible only by carefully observing oneself.

To flee the work of inner observation, to seek evasions, is an unmistakable sign of degeneration.

Obviously, the goal of this work is precisely to achieve a gradual change in our internal life. Yet, as long as a human being holds onto the illusion that he is one and the same person, he cannot change.

Radical transformation is a defined possibility, which is normally lost when one does not work on oneself.

The initial point of radical change remains hidden as long as the person continues believing himself to be one.

Those who reject the Doctrine of the Many "I's" are clearly demonstrating that they have never observed themselves seriously.

The severe observation of the "myself," without subterfuges of any type, permits us to verify by ourselves the crude reality that we are not "one" but "many."

Amidst the subjective opinions of this world, the diverse pseudo-esoteric or pseudo-occultist theories always become an alley we use to flee from ourselves...

Unquestionably, the illusion that one is always one and the same person serves as a hidden obstacle for self-observation...

Someone could say, "I know that I am not one but many; Gnosis taught me this." Yet, if there is not a fully lived experience regarding this aspect of the doctrine, then such an affirmation, even if very sincere, would obviously be something merely external and superficial.

Therefore, what is fundamental is to perceive, to experience and to comprehend. Only thus is it possible to work consciously in order to achieve a radical change.

Hence, affirming is one thing and comprehending is another. When someone says, "I comprehend that I am not one but many," if this comprehension is authentic and not merely insubstantial, vain wordiness of ambiguous chattering, then this indicates, points out, declares a full verification of the Doctrine of the Many "I's."

Knowledge and comprehension are different. Knowledge is of the mind. Comprehension is of the heart.

Therefore, the mere knowledge of the Doctrine of the Many "I's" is good for nothing. Unfortunately, in these times in which we live, knowledge has gone far beyond comprehension. This is because the wretched intellectual animal, mistakenly called the human being, exclusively developed the side of knowledge, lamentably forgetting the corresponding side of the Being.

To know the Doctrine of the Many "I's" and to comprehend it is fundamental for any true radical change.

When a person begins to observe his inner self in detail, from the angle that he is not one but many, it is obvious that he has initiated a serious work upon his inner nature.

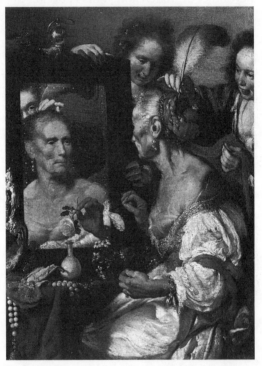

VANITAS ALLEGORY BY BERNARDO STROZZI, 1635.

Chapter 13

The Observer and the Observed

It is very clear and not difficult to comprehend that when one seriously begins to observe oneself from the point of view that the "myself" is not "one" but "many," one then really begins to work on all that is carried within.

Hindrances, obstacles, stumbling blocks for the work of intimate self-observation, such are the following psychological defects:

> **Megalomania:** delusions of grandeur, to believe that one is a God.
>
> **Self-worship:** belief in a permanent "I," adoration of any type of alter-ego.
>
> **Paranoia:** know-it all ignoramus, self-sufficiency, vanity, thinking oneself infallible, mystical pride, a person who does not like to see another person's point of view.

When an individual continues with the absurd conviction that myself is "one," that such a person possesses a permanent "I," then the serious work upon oneself becomes more than impossible.

Whosoever always considers himself as "one" will never be able to separate the self from his own undesirable elements. Such a person will consider each thought, sentiment, desire, emotion, passion, affection, etc. as different and unchangeable functionalisms of his own nature and will even justify himself before others saying that such and such personal defects are of a hereditary nature.

Whosoever accepts the Doctrine of the Many "I's," based on self-observation, comprehends that every desire, thought, action, passion, etc., corresponds to this or that "I," meaning, to a distinct or different "I."

Whosoever works very seriously on himself, as any athlete of inner self-observation, exerts upon himself the effort to separate from his psyche the diverse undesirable elements which he carries within...

Thus, if one truly and very sincerely begins to observe oneself internally, one ends up dividing himself in two: the observer and the observed.

If such a division is not produced, it is then evident that we would never take a step forward in the marvelous pathway of self-knowledge.

How can we observe ourselves if we commit the error of not wanting to divide ourselves into observer and the observed?

If such a division is not produced, it is obvious that we will never take a step forward upon the path of self-knowledge.

Undoubtedly, when this division does not occur, we then continue identified with all the processes of the pluralized "I."

Whosoever identifies himself with the diverse processes of the pluralized "I" is always a victim of circumstances.

How could the one who does not know himself modify circumstances? How could a person who has never observed himself internally know himself? In what way can someone observe himself if this one, first of all, does not divide himself into observer and observed?

Now then, no one can start to change radically as long as such a one is incapable of saying, "This desire is an animal "I" which I must eliminate," "This egotistical thought is another "I" that torments me and that I need to disintegrate," "This sentiment that hurts my heart is an intruding "I," which I need to reduce to cosmic dust," etc.

Naturally, the statements of the former paragraph are impossible to say for the one who has never divided himself between observer and observed.

Whosoever takes all his psychological processes as functionalisms of a unique, individual and permanent "I" is identified with all his errors. He has them so tied to himself that he has lost the capacity to separate them from his psyche.

Obviously, people like that can never change radically; they are people condemned to the most complete failure.

Chapter 14
Negative Thoughts

In this devolving and decadent era, it is unusual for anyone to think with profundity and with full attention.

Diverse thoughts surge from the intellectual center, not from a permanent "I," as the learned ignoramuses foolishly assume, but from the different "I's" in each of us.

When a person is thinking, he firmly believes that he is the one who is thinking in himself and by himself.

The wretched intellectual mammal does not want to realize that the multiple thoughts that cross his mind have their origin in the different "I's" which we carry within.

This signifies that we are not true thinking individuals. Indeed, we do not yet have an individual mind.

However, each of the different "I's" that we carry within utilizes our intellectual center. At any time, as often as possible, each of them utilizes the intellectual center in order to think.

Therefore, to identify ourselves
with this or that negative and harmful
thought, believing it to be our particular
property, would be an absurdity.

Obviously, this or that negative
thought proceeds from any "I," which in
a given moment has abusively used our
intellectual center.

There are different types of negative
thoughts, namely: suspicion, distrust,
ill-will towards another person, passionate jealousy, religious jealousy, political
jealousy, family or friendship jealousy,
covetousness, lust, revenge, anger, pride,
envy, hatred, resentment, theft, adultery,
laziness, gluttony, etc.

Indeed, we could not succeed in enu-
merating all the psychological defects we
have since they are too many, not even
if we had a steel palate and a thousand
tongues to speak.

Therefore, and as a corollary to the former statement, to identify with negative
thoughts is an absurdity.

Since it is impossible for there to be an
effect without a cause, we solemnly affirm
that a thought could never exist by itself,
by spontaneous generation...

The relation between thinker and thought is obvious. Each negative thought has its origin in a different thinker.

There are many negative thinkers within each one of us, as many thoughts of the same class.

Examining this subject matter from the pluralized angle of "thinkers and thoughts," it is understood then that each one of the "I's" that we carry in our psyche is certainly a different thinker.

Unquestionably, there are too many thinkers inside each one of us. Nonetheless, each one of these inner-thinkers, in spite of being merely one part, believes himself to be the whole, at any given moment...

The mythomaniacs, megalomaniacs, ego worshippers, narcissists and paranoid ones would never accept the thesis of the "plurality of thinkers," because they love themselves too much. They believe themselves to be "Superman's daddy" or "Wonder Woman's mommy."

How could such abnormal people accept the idea that they do not possess an individual, brilliant and marvelous mind?

Nevertheless, those know-it-all ignora-muses think the best of themselves and even wear the robe of Aristippus in order to demonstrate wisdom and humility...

It is stated, in accordance with ancient legend, that Aristippus wanted to demon-strate wisdom and humility. So, he decked himself with an old robe full of patches and holes, then held the rod of philoso-phy with his right hand and walked the streets of Athens... When Socrates saw him coming, he exclaimed in a loud voice: "Oh Aristippus, your vanity is shown through the holes of your vesture."

The one who unceasingly does not live in a state of alert novelty, alert percep-tion, thinking that he is thinking, easily becomes identified with any negative thought.

Thus, lamentably, as an outcome of his behavior, he strengthens the disas-trous power of the "negative I" who is the author of the corresponding thought in question.

The more we identify ourselves with a negative thought, the more we shall be slaves of the corresponding "I" that char-acterizes it.

Regarding Gnosis, the secret path, and the work upon oneself, our own particular temptations are precisely found in those "I's" who hate Gnosis, who hate the esoteric work. These "I's" do not ignore that their existence within our psyche is mortally threatened by Gnosis and by this work.

Those quarrelsome and negative "I's" easily take control of certain mental films that are stored in our intellectual center, which sequentially originate harmful and noxious mental currents.

If we accept those thoughts, those negative "I's," which at any given moment control our intellectual center, we shall then be incapable of freeing ourselves from their influence.

We must never forget that every negative "I" deceives itself and betrays to that end; it lies.

Each time that one feels a sudden loss of strength, when the aspirant becomes disillusioned about Gnosis, about the esoteric work, when one loses the enthusiasm and abandons what is best, it is obvious that one has been deceived by some negative "I."

The negative "I" of jealousy deceives those beings who adore each other and destroys their happiness.

The negative "I" of mystical pride deceives the devotees of the path. Thus, believing themselves to be wise, they despise their master[3] and betray him...

The negative "I" appeals to our personal experiences, our memories, our best wishes, our sincerity. Hence, amidst all of these things, through a rigorous selection, this negative "I" presents something under a false light, something that fascinates. Thus, the outcome is failure...

Nonetheless, when one discovers that "I" in action, when one has learned to live in a state of alertness, then such a deception becomes impossible.

---

3   "...we state that there is only one master; this is the inner Christ that enlightens every human being who comes into the world. Thus, only Christ is the master. Only the resplendent "I Am" is the master." —Samael Aun Weor, *Major Mysteries*

Chapter 15

Individuality

Indeed, to believe that we are "one" is a joke made in very bad taste. Unfortunately, this vain illusion exists within each one of us.

It is unfortunate that we always think the best of ourselves. It never occurs to us to comprehend that we do not even possess true individuality.

The worst of the matter is that we give ourselves the false luxury of assuming that each one of us enjoys full consciousness and a will of our own.

Woe to us! What nitwits we are! There is no doubt that ignorance is the worst of all disgraces.

Many thousands of different individuals, different persons, "I's," or people who quarrel amongst themselves, who fight amongst themselves for supremacy and who do not have order or concordance whatsoever, exist within each one of us.

If we were conscious, if we were to awaken from so many dreams and fantasies, how different life would be...

Nonetheless, as if our misfortune was not enough, negative emotions, self-love and self-esteem fascinate us, hypnotize us, never allowing us to remember ourselves, to see ourselves exactly the way we are...

We believe that we have one will, when in reality we possess many different wills. Each "I" has its own will.

The tragic comedy of all this interior multiplicity is dreadful. The different internal wills clash against each other, they live in continuous conflict, and they act in different directions.

If we had true individuality, if we were a unity instead of a multiplicity, then we would also have continuity of purpose, awakened consciousness, a particular, individual will.

To change is the best; however, we must begin by being sincere with ourselves.

We need to make a psychological inventory of ourselves in order to know what we have in excess or what we lack.

To attain individuality is possible, yet if we believe that we already have it, then such a possibility will disappear.

It is evident that we would never struggle to obtain individuality if we believe that we already have it. Fantasy makes us believe that we are possessors of individuality and there are even schools in the world that teach it that way.

To struggle against fantasy is urgent. Fantasy makes us appear as if we were this or that, when, indeed, we are miserable, shameless and perverse.

We think that we are humans, when in truth we are merely intellectual mammals lacking individuality.

Megalomaniacs believe themselves to be gods, Mahatmas, etc., without even suspecting that they do not even have an individual mind and conscious will.

Ego worshippers adore their beloved ego so much that they would never accept the multiplicity of egos within themselves.

Paranoids, with all the classic pride that characterizes them, will not even read this book...

It is indispensable to fight to death against the fantasy regarding our own selves, if we do not want to be victims of artificial emotions and false experiences. This is because fantasy, besides placing us in ridiculous situations, stops all possibility of internal development.

The intellectual animal is so hypnotized by his fantasy, that he dreams that he is a lion or eagle when in truth he is nothing more than a vile slug from the mud of the earth.

The megalomaniac would never accept these afore-mentioned affirmations. Obviously, regardless of what people might say, he feels himself to be an Archhierophant, without suspecting that fantasy is merely nothing. "Fantasy is nothing but fantasy."

Fantasy is a real force which acts universally upon mankind. It keeps the intellectual humanoid in a state of sleep (hypnotic state), causing him to believe that he is already a human being, that he possesses true individuality, a will, awakened consciousness and a mind of his own, etc.

When we think that we are "one," we cannot move from where we are within ourselves; thus, we remain stagnant, and lastly, we degenerate, we devolve.

Each one of us is situated in a determined psychological phase. We cannot remove ourselves from within this psychological state unless we directly discover all those persons or "I's" who live within our own person.

It is clear that only through inner self-observation shall we be able to see the people who live in our psyche and who we need to eliminate in order to achieve a radical transformation.

This perception, this self-observation, fundamentally alters all the mistaken concepts that we had regarding ourselves; thus, as an outcome, we witness the concrete fact that we do not possess true individuality.

Therefore, as long as we do not observe ourselves, we will then live in the illusion that we are "one," and consequently our life will be a mistake.

To correctly relate with our fellowmen would be impossible as long as we do not perform an internal change in the very core of our psyche.

Any internal change demands the previous elimination of the "I's" that we carry within.

We cannot, by any means, eliminate such "I's" if we do not internally observe them.

Those who consider themselves "one," those who think the best of themselves, those who would never accept the Doctrine of the Many, will never desire to observe their "I's." Therefore, within them, any possibility of change will be impossible.

It is not possible to change if one does not eliminate; yet, whosoever considers himself a possessor of individuality, even if he would accept that he must eliminate, would indeed ignore what it is that he must eliminate.

Nonetheless, we must not forget that whosoever believes himself to be "one" will deceive himself, thinking that he does know that which he must eliminate. Yet, indeed, he does not even know that he does not know; he is a learned ignoramus.

We need to "de-egotize" ourselves so we can "individualize" ourselves; however, to "de-egotize" is impossible for the one who thinks that he possesses individuality.

Individuality is one hundred percent sacred; rare are those who have it, nevertheless everyone thinks they have it.

How can we eliminate "I's" if we think that we have a unique "I"?

Certainly, only the one who has never seriously observed his own self can think that he has a unique "I."

Nevertheless, in regard to this teaching, we must be very clear, because the psychological danger of confusing authentic individuality with the concept of some species of a "superior I," or something similar, exists.

Sacred individuality is very far beyond any type of "I." Sacred individuality is what it is, what it has always been and what it shall always be.

Legitimate individuality is the Being. The reason for the Being to be is to be the Being Himself.

Distinguish between the Being and the "I." Those who confuse the "I" with the Being have certainly never observed themselves seriously.

As long as the Essence, the consciousness, is bottled up within all of that conjunction of "I's" that we carry inside, radical change will be something more than impossible.

Neither Beginning nor End

The End is swallowed up by the
Beginning.

Chapter 16

The Book of Life

A person is what his life is. That which continues beyond death is life. This is the meaning of the book of life that opens with death.

When this subject matter is contemplated from a strictly psychological point of view, indeed, a routine day of our life is just a small replica of the totality of our life.

Therefore, as an outcome of all of this, we can infer the following: if a human being does not work on himself today, he will never change.

When one affirms that one wants to work on himself, and he does not work today, putting it off for tomorrow, such an affirmation will be a simple project and nothing more, because in it is a replica of all our life.

There is a common saying that states, "Do not leave for tomorrow what you can do today."

If a human being says, "I will work on myself tomorrow," then he will never work on himself, because there will always be a tomorrow.

This is very similar to a certain sign, notice or poster that some merchants put in their stores, "I do not give credit today, but I will tomorrow."

When any penniless person arrives asking for credit, he comes upon this terrible sign and if he returns the next day, once more he finds this wretched notice or poster.

This is what in psychology is called the "sickness of tomorrow." As long as a person says "tomorrow," he will never change.

We need, with maximum urgency, to work on ourselves and not dream lazily of a future or any extraordinary opportunity.

Those who say, "I will first do this or that and then work," will never work on themselves. They are "the dwellers of the earth" mentioned in the holy scriptures.

I knew a powerful landlord that used to say, "First of all, I need to be well-off, then I will work on myself."

When I visited him on his deathbed, I then asked him the following question, "Do you still want to be well-off?"

He answered me, "I truly lament having wasted my time." He died some days later, after having acknowledged his mistake. That man had many lands; however, he wanted to own the neighboring properties so that he could become "well-off," so that his estate would be bordered exactly by four roads.

The great Kabir Jesus said,

> "Sufficient unto the day [is] the evil thereof." —Christian Bible, Matthew 6:34

Let us observe ourselves today, in whatever concerns the ever-recurring day, which is a miniature of our entire life.

When a human being begins to work on his own self, here and now, today, when he observes his displeasure and pain, he then walks upon the path of success.

It is impossible to eliminate what we do not know. Therefore, we must first observe our own errors.

We need not only to observe our day, but also our relationship to it. A certain ordinary day that each person experiences directly exists, with the exception of unusual and uncommon incidents.

So, it is interesting to observe daily recurrence, the repetition of words and events towards each person, etc.

That repetition or recurrence of events and words deserves to be studied; it leads us to self-knowledge.

Chapter 17

Mechanical Creatures

By no means can we deny that the law of recurrence processes itself in every moment of our life.

Indeed, in each day of our existence, there are repetitions of events, states of consciousness, words, desires, thoughts, volitions, etc.

It is obvious that when one does not observe oneself, one cannot observe this incessant daily repetition.

It is evident that whosoever does not have any interest in observing himself also does not desire to work in order to achieve a true radical transformation.

To top it all off, there are people who want to transform themselves without working on themselves.

We do not deny the fact that each person has a right to the true happiness of the Spirit. Nonetheless, it is also true that such happiness would be more than impossible if we do not work on ourselves.

When one truly manages to modify his reactions against the diverse happenings that occur daily, one can then change intimately.

However, we could not change our way of reacting to the facts of practical life, if we do not work seriously upon ourselves.

We need to change our way of thinking. We need to be less negligent. We need to become more serious and to face life in a different manner. We need to face life in its real and practical sense.

However, if we continue the way we are, behaving the same way everyday, repeating the same errors, repeating the same negligence as always, then indeed any possibility of change will be eliminated.

If one truly wants to know oneself, one must then begin by observing his own conduct while facing the events of any day of his life.

We do not want to imply by this that one must not observe oneself daily. We only state that self-observation begins with the first day that one starts observing oneself.

There must be a beginning in everything; thus, to start by observing our conduct in any given day of our life is a good beginning.

Certainly, the most appropriate beginning is to observe our mechanical reactions when facing all those small details at home, in the bedroom, in the dining room, in the house, on the street, at work, etc., what we say, feel and think.

Then, what is important is to see how or in what manner we can change these mechanical reactions. However, we will never change if we think that we are good persons, that we never behave in an unconscious and mistaken manner.

First of all, we need to comprehend that we are machine-persons, simple marionettes controlled by secret agents, by hidden "I's."

Many people live inside of us; we are never identical. Sometimes, a selfish person manifests through us, other times an irritable person, in any other instant, a generous, benevolent person, later on a scandalous one, a slanderous person, afterwards a saint, then, a liar, etc.

Thus, inside of each one of us we have people of all types, "I's" of all species. Our personality is nothing more than a marionette, a talking doll, something mechanical.

Let us start by acting consciously during a small portion of our day. We need to stop being simple machines, even if it is for at least a few brief daily minutes. This will have a decisive influence on our existence.

When we observe ourselves and do not do what this or that "I" wants us to do, then it is clear that we begin to stop being machines.

A single moment in which one is sufficiently conscious as to stop being a machine, if it is done with will, tends to radically modify many disagreeable circumstances.

Unfortunately, we live daily a mechanical, routine and absurd life. We repeat occurrences; our habits are the same; we never want to modify them. They are the mechanical tracks on which circulates the train of our miserable existence. Nevertheless, we think the best of ourselves.

"Megalomaniacs" abound everywhere. Those who think themselves to be gods, nonetheless, are mechanical routine creatures, people from the mud of the earth, wretched dolls moved by diverse "I's."

People like this will never work upon
themselves.

The Christ gives the bread (knowledge)
to the repentant soul.

THE COMMUNION OF THE APOSTLES BY JUSEPE DE RIBERA, 1651.

Chapter 18

The Supersubstantial Bread

If we carefully observe any day of our life, we will see that we certainly do not know how to live consciously.

Our life seems like a train in motion, moving upon the fixed tracks of the mechanical and rigid habits of a vain and superficial existence.

The intriguing aspect of this matter is that it never occurs to us to modify habits. It seems that we never get weary of always repeating the same thing.

We have become petrified by our habits, nevertheless we think that we are free. We are dreadfully ugly, yet we think of ourselves as Apollo.

We are mechanical people. This mechanicity is more than enough motive to deprive us of any true sensibility in regard to what we are doing in life.

We move daily on our old track, inside of our antiquated and absurd shuttle of habits; thus, it is clear that we do not have a real life. Instead of living, we vegetate miserably and we do not receive new impressions.

If a person begins his day consciously, then it is evident that such a day would be very different compared to other days.

When the day one is living is taken as the totality of one's life, when one does not leave for tomorrow what one must do this very day, then indeed one gets to know what the work on oneself really means.

A day never lacks importance; therefore, if we really want to transform ourselves radically, we must then see, observe and comprehend ourselves daily.

Nonetheless, people do not want to see their selves in themselves. Some of them, in spite of having desires to work on themselves, justify their negligence with phrases like the following, "The work in the office does not allow me to work on myself." These empty, vain and absurd words, without any sense, only serve in order to justify indolence, laziness and lack of love for the "Great Cause."

Obviously, people like these, although they may have great spiritual longings, will never change.

To observe ourselves is something unavoidable and non-excludable, since intimate self-observation is fundamental for a true change.

What is your psychological state when you get out of bed? What is the level of your emotional mood during breakfast? Were you impatient with the waiter? With your wife? Why were you impatient? What is that which always disturbs you, etc.?

Smoking less or eating less is not a complete change; yet, indeed it indicates a certain progress. We know very well that vice and gluttony are inhumane and bestial.

It is not right that someone who devotes his/her self to the secret path has a physical body that is excessively fat with a protruding abdomen. This is totally out of harmonious perfection. This would indicate gluttony and even laziness.

Even though everyday life, profession, work are vital for our existence, they constitute, nonetheless, the sleepy state of our consciousness.

To know that life is a dream does not mean that we have comprehended it. Comprehension is attained through self-observation and intense work on oneself.

Hence, in order to work on oneself, it is indispensable to work on one's daily life, this very day. Thus, one will comprehend that phrase from the Prayer of the Lord (Pater Noster) which states, "Give us this day our daily bread."

The phrase "daily bread" means the "supersubstantial bread" in Greek or the "bread from the Highest."

Gnosis gives us this "bread of life" in a double meaning; this is ideas and strength, which allow us to disintegrate our psychological errors.

We gain psychological experience, we eat the "bread of wisdom," and we receive new knowledge every time that we reduce to cosmic dust this or that "I."

Gnosis offers the "supersubstantial bread," the "bread of knowledge," thus indicating to us with precision the new life that begins in oneself, inside oneself, here and now.

Now then, no one can alter his life or change anything related with mechanical reactions unless one can count on the help of new ideas and receive divine help.

Gnosis gives those new ideas and points out the "modus operandi" by which one can be assisted by forces superior to the mind.

We need to prepare the inferior centers of our organism in order to receive the ideas and forces that come from the superior centers.

In the work on oneself, there is nothing worthless. Any thought, however insignificant it might be, deserves to be observed. Any negative emotion, reaction, etc. must be observed.

HERMES / MERCURY

"Whosoever wants to truly achieve the development of the Essence in themselves must become hermetically sealed."

Chapter 19

The Good Master
of the House

Indeed, to detach oneself from the
disastrous effects of life in these tenebrous times is very difficult, but indispensable. Otherwise, one is devoured by
life.

Any work that one does on oneself
with the purpose of achieving a spiritual
and psychic development is always related
with a very well understood type of isola-
tion. This is because the personality is the
only thing that one can develop under the
influence of life as we have always lived it;
anything else is impossible.

We do not intend to oppose the development of the personality in any way.
Obviously this is necessary in life. Yet,
indeed the personality is merely something artificial. The personality is neither
the truth nor the reality in us.

If the wretched intellectual mammals,
mistakenly called human beings, do not
isolate themselves, but identify with all
the occurrences of practical life, if they

waste their strength in negative emotions, in personal self-consideration and in insubstantial vain wordiness of ambiguous chattering, then nothing constructive, no real element can be developed within them, except that which belongs to this world of mechanicity.

Indeed, whosoever wants to truly achieve the development of the Essence in themselves must become hermetically sealed. This statement refers to something intimate, closely related to silence.

The phrase "hermetically sealed" comes from ancient times when a doctrine on the internal development of a human being associated with the name of Hermes was secretly taught.

Therefore, if we want something real to grow within our interior, it is evident that we must avoid the escape of our psychic energies.

When our energies drain away and we are not inwardly isolated, then it is unquestionable that we will not be able to attain the development of something real within our psyche.

Ordinary routine life wants to devour us mercilessly. Hence, we must fight against life daily; we must learn to swim against the current.

This work goes against daily life. It deals with something very different from that of daily life and something that we must, nonetheless, practice from moment to moment. I am referring to the revolution of the consciousness.

Evidently, if our attitude towards daily life is fundamentally mistaken, if we believe that everything should turn out well because that is the way it is supposed to be, then we will be disappointed.

People want things to turn out well, "because that is the way it is meant to be," because everything should be in accordance with their plans. Nevertheless, crude reality is different; therefore, as long as one does not change internally, whether we like it or not, we will be a victim of circumstances.

Many sentimental stupidities are uttered and written about life. Yet, this *Treatise of Revolutionary Psychology* is different. This doctrine goes straight to the point, to concrete, clear and definite facts. This doctrine emphatically affirms that the "intellectual animal," mistakenly called a human being, is a mechanical, unconscious, sleeping biped.

"The good master of the house" will never accept revolutionary psychology. "The good master of the house" fulfills all his duties as father, husband, etc., and because of it, thinks the best of himself. Nonetheless, he only serves Nature's ends. That is all.

On the other hand, we shall state that "the good master of the house" who swims against the current, who does not want to be devoured by life, also exists. However, this type of individual is very rare in the world. There are very few of this type.

When one behaves in accordance with the ideas of this *Treatise of Revolutionary Psychology,* one obtains an upright perception of life.

Chapter 20

The Two Worlds

To observe and to self-observe oneself are two completely different things; however, both demand attention.

When we observe through the windows of the senses, our attention then is directed outwardly towards the external world.

Yet, in self-observation, the senses of external perception are worthless, because attention is directed inward. Consequently, this is the factual reason why the self-observation of inner psychological processes is difficult for the neophyte.

The point of departure of official science in its practical side is the observable. The point of departure for the work on oneself is self-observation, the self-observable.

Unquestionably, these two points of departure take us in two completely different directions.

Someone could grow old engrossed within the intransigent dogmas of official science, studying external phenomena, observing cells, atoms, molecules, suns, stars, comets, etc., without experiencing any radical change within himself.

The type of knowledge that transforms someone internally can never be achieved through external observation.

The true knowledge that can really originate a fundamental, internal change in us has as its basis direct self-observation of oneself.

We urgently need to encourage our Gnostic students to observe themselves and in what manner they must observe themselves and the reasons for this.

Observation is a way to modify the mechanical conditions of the world. Yet, internal self-observation is a way to intimately change.

Consequently, and as a corollary to the former statement, we can and must emphatically affirm that there are two types of knowledge: the external and the internal. Therefore, if we do not have within ourselves the magnetic center that can differentiate between these two qualities of knowledge, then confusion would be the only outcome of this mixture of two canons or orders of ideas.

Sublime pseudo-esoteric doctrines with marked scientism at heart belong to the field of the externally observable. Nevertheless, they are accepted by many aspirants as internal knowledge.

We find ourselves then before two worlds, the external and the internal.

The first, the external, is perceived by the senses of external perception. The second, the internal, can only be perceived through the sense of internal self-observation.

Thoughts, ideas, emotions, longings, hopes, disappointments, etc., are internal, invisible to the ordinary, common and current senses. Yet, they are more real to us than the dining table or the living room couch.

Indeed, we live in our internal world more than in our external world. This is irrefutable, indisputable.

In our internal worlds, in our secret world, we love, desire, suspect, bless, curse, yearn, suffer, enjoy, we are disappointed, rewarded, etc.

Unquestionably, the two worlds, internal and external, are experimentally verifiable. The external world is the observable. The internal world is in itself and inside oneself the self-observable, here and now.

Whosoever truly wants to know the internal worlds of the planet Earth or of the solar system or of the galaxy in which we live, must previously know their intimate world, their individual, internal life, their own internal worlds.

> *"Human, know thyself, and thou wilt know the universe and its gods."*

The more we explore this internal world called "myself," the more we will comprehend that we simultaneously live in two worlds, in two realities, in two confines: the external and the internal.

In the same way that it is indispensable for one to learn how to walk in the external world so as not to fall down into a precipice, or not get lost in the streets of the city, or to select one's friends, or not associate with the perverse ones, or not eat poison, etc.; likewise, through the psychological work upon oneself, we learn how to walk in the internal world, which is explorable only through self-observation.

Indeed, the sense of self-observation is atrophied in this decadent human race of this tenebrous era in which we live.

As we persevere in self-observation, the sense of intimate self-observation will progressively develop.

ETCHING BY FRANCISCO GOYA. "THE SLEEP OF REASON PRODUCES MONSTERS."

"Unquestionably, as long as the Essence or
consciousness continues bottled up within each
one of the "I's" that we carry within our interior,
it will always be asleep, in a subconscious state."

Chapter 21

Observation of Oneself

Internal self-observation is a practical means to achieve a radical transformation.

To know and to observe are different. Many confuse the observation of oneself with knowing. For example, even though we know that we are seated in a living room, this, however, does not signify that we are observing the chair.

We know that at a given moment we are in a negative state, perhaps with a problem, worried about this or that matter, or in a state of distress or uncertainty, etc. This, however, does not mean that we are observing the negative state.

Do you feel antipathy towards someone? Do you dislike a certain person? Why? You may say that you know that person... Please observe that person; to know is not the same as to observe! Do not confuse knowing with observing...

The observation of oneself, which is one hundred percent active, is a way to change oneself. However, knowing, which is passive, is not a way to change oneself.

Indeed, knowing is not an act of attention. Yet, the attention directed into oneself, towards what is happening in our interior, is something positive, active...

For instance, we may feel antipathy towards a person, just because we feel like it and many times for no particular reason. If we observe ourselves in such a moment we will notice the multitude of thoughts that accumulate in our mind. We will also notice the group of voices that speak and scream in a disorderly manner and that say many things within our mind, as well as the unpleasant emotions that surge in our interior and the unpleasant taste that all this leaves in our psyche, etc.

Obviously, in such a state we also realize that internally we are badly mistreating the person towards whom we feel antipathy.

But, unquestionably, in order to see all of this, we need attention intentionally directed towards the interior of our own selves. This is not a passive attention.

Indeed, dynamic attention proceeds from the side of the observer, while thoughts and emotions belong to the side which is observed.

All of this causes us to comprehend that "knowing" is something completely passive and mechanical, in evident contrast with the observation of the self, which is a conscious act.

Nevertheless, we are not affirming that mechanical self-observation does not exist; it does, but such a kind of observation has nothing to do with the psychological self-observation to which we are referring.

To think and to observe are also very different. Any person can give themselves the luxury of thinking about themselves all they want, yet this does not signify that they are is truly observing themselves.

We need to see the different "I's" in action, to discover them in our psyche, to comprehend that a percentage of our consciousness is within each of them, to repent of having created them, etc.

Then we shall exclaim, "But what is this "I" doing?" "What is it saying?" "What does it want?" "Why does it torment me with its lust, with its anger?" etc.

Then we will see within ourselves the entire train of thoughts, emotions, desires, passions, private comedies, personal dramas, elaborated lies, discourses, excuses, morbidities, beds of pleasure, scenes of lasciviousness, etc.

Many times before falling asleep, at the precise instant of transition between vigil and sleep, we feel within our mind different voices that talk to each other. Those are the different "I's" that must in such moments break all connection with the different centers of our organic machine, so as to then submerge themselves in the molecular world, within the "fifth dimension."

Chapter 22
Chatter

It is urgent, unavoidable and non-excludable to observe our internal chatter and its precise place of origin.

Unquestionably, many present as well as future disharmonious and unpleasant psychic states have their *causa causorum* in our erroneous internal chatter.

Obviously, all that insubstantial, vain wordiness of ambiguous chattering and all harmful, damaging and absurd jabber in general, uttered in this external world, has its origin in our wrong internal gibberish.

There is an esoteric exercise of internal silence in Gnosis. Our disciples in "Third Chamber" know of it. It is not irrelevant to state with complete clarity that internal silence must specifically refer to something precise and definite. This internal silence is achieved when the process of thinking is intentionally exhausted during profound inner meditation. Nevertheless, this is not what we want to explain in the present chapter.

"To empty the mind" or "to make it blank" in order to achieve internal silence is not what we want to explain in these paragraphs either.

The practice of internal silence to which we are referring does not mean to impede something from penetrating into the mind either.

Indeed, right now we are talking about something very different, a different kind of internal silence. This is not something vague and ordinary...

The internal silence that we want to exercise is related with something that is already in our mind: a person, event, our business or another one's business, what we were told, what such a fellow did, etc., without our interior tongue commenting about these things, without internal discourse...

To learn how to remain silent not only with the exterior tongue, but also with the secret, internal tongue, is something extraordinary and marvelous.

Many keep quiet externally; however, with their internal tongue they skin their fellow men alive. The internal, poisonous and malevolent chatter produces inner confusion.

If one observes wrong internal chatter, one will then see that it is made up of half-truths or of truths that are more or less incorrectly related to each other, or of things that were added or omitted.

Unfortunately, our emotional life is exclusively based on "self-sympathy."

To top off so much infamy, we only sympathize with ourselves, with our much "beloved ego." Moreover, we feel antipathy and even hatred towards those who do not sympathize with us.

We love ourselves too much. We are one hundred percent narcissists; this is irrefutable, indisputable.

As long as we continue bottled up in "self-sympathy," any development of the Being becomes something more than impossible.

We need to learn to see others' points of view. It is urgent to know how to place ourselves in the place of others.

> *"Therefore, all things whatsoever ye would that men should do to you, do ye even so to them."*
> —Christian Bible, Matthew 7:12

What truly counts in these studies is the manner in which human beings behave internally and invisibly with one another.

Unfortunately, and even if we were very courteous and even sincere at times, there is no doubt that invisibly and internally we treat each other very badly.

People who are apparently very generous drag their fellow men daily into the secret caves of themselves to do with them whatever they please (abuse, mockery, contempt, etc.).

Chapter 23

The World of Relations

The world of relationships has three very different aspects that we need to clarify in a precise manner.

First: We are related with the planetary body, in other words, the physical body.

Second: We live on the planet Earth and by logical consequence we are related with the exterior world and with our personal matters such as relatives, business, money, office matters, profession, politics, etc.

Third: We have the relationship of a person with himself. For the majority of people, this kind of relationship does not have the least importance.

Unfortunately, people are only interested in the first two kinds of relationships. They look at the third type with the most absolute indifference.

Indeed, nourishment, health, money and business constitute the principal worries of the "intellectual animal" mistakenly called the "human being."

Now then, it is evident that the physical body, as well as worldly matters, are exterior to ourselves.

The planetary body (physical body) is sometimes sick, sometimes healthy and so on.

We always believe that we have some knowledge of our physical body; yet indeed, not even the best scientists of the world know much about the body of flesh and bone.

There is no doubt that the physical body, given its tremendous and complex organization, is certainly much beyond our comprehension.

Regarding the second type of relationship, we are always victims of circumstances. It is lamentable that we have not yet learned how to consciously originate circumstances.

Many are the people who are incapable of adapting themselves to anything or anyone or to have true success in life.

When we think in ourselves in relation with the Gnostic esoteric work, it is then

imperative to discover if we are at fault
with any of these three types of relationships.

A concrete case can come to pass that
we become physically ill, as a consequence
of being incorrectly related with our physical bodies.

It can happen that we are incorrectly
related with the exterior world. Thus, as a
result, we have conflicts, economical and
social problems, etc.

It can come to pass that we are incorrectly related with ourselves. Accordingly,
we suffer deeply due to the lack of inner
enlightenment.

Obviously, if the lamp of our room is
not connected to the electrical installa-
tion, our room will be in darkness.

Therefore, those who suffer from a
lack of inner illumination must connect
their mind with the superior centers of
their Being.

Unquestionably, we need to establish
correct relationships not only with our
planetary body (physical body) and with
the exterior world but also with each of
the parts of our own Being.

Pessimistic patients, tired of so many
doctors and medicines, no longer desire

to be cured. Yet, optimistic patients struggle to live.

Many millionaires who lose their fortune gambling in the casino of Monte Carlo commit suicide, while millions of poor mothers work to maintain their children.

Innumerable are the depressed aspirants who, due to a lack of psychic powers and inner illumination, have renounced the esoteric work for themselves.

Few are those who know how to take advantage of adversities.

During times of rigorous temptations, discouragement and desolation, one must appeal to the intimate Remembering of the Self.

Deep within each one of us is the Aztec Tonantzin, Stella Maris, the Egyptian Isis, God the Mother, waiting for us in order to heal our painful heart.

When one gives to oneself the shock of "Self-remembering," then indeed, a miraculous change in the entire work of the body is produced, so that the cells receive a different nourishment.

Chapter 24

The Psychological Song

The moment in order to very seriously reflect about that which is called "internal consideration" has arrived.

There is not the least bit of doubt regarding the disastrous consequences of "intimate self-consideration." Besides hypnotizing the consciousness, it causes us to lose a lot of energy.

If one would not make the mistake of identifying too much with one's self, then internal self-consideration would be something more than impossible.

When one becomes identified with his "self," such a one loves his own self too much and feels self-pity. Often, such a person thinks that he has always behaved very well with this or that fellow, with the spouse, children, etc. and that nobody has appreciated it, etc. In sum, one is a saint and all others are scoundrels and rascals.

Preoccupation about what others might think about our own selves is one of the most common forms of inner self-consideration. They might suppose that

we are not honest, sincere, truthful, cou-
rageous, etc.

The most intriguing aspect of all this
subject matter is that we unfortunately
ignore the enormous loss of energy that
this kind of worrying causes us.

Precisely such worries born from our
inner self-consideration are the cause of
many hostile attitudes towards certain
persons who have done us no evil.

In these circumstances, loving oneself
too much, considering oneself in this way,
it is clear that the "I," or better if we say
the "I's," instead of disappearing, become
horribly fortified.

A person who is identified with his
"self" pities his own situation, and it
even occurs to him to keep a count of his
problems.

This is why he thinks, in spite of all
his well-known generosities, this or that
fellow, the godfather, godmother, the
neighbor, the boss, the friend, etc. have
not repaid him as they were supposed
to. Therefore, bottled up within this, he
becomes unbearable and boring to the
entire world.

Practically, one cannot talk with such
a person, because any conversation will

certainly end up in his accounting book of such boastful sufferings.

Regarding the Gnostic esoteric work, it is written that the growth of one's soul is only possible through the forgiveness of others.

If someone lives from instant to instant, from moment to moment, suffering because he feels that others owe him something, because others have mistreated him, because others have caused him bitterness, then nothing will be able to grow in his interior, because he will always sing the same song.

The Lord's Prayer says, "Forgive us our trespasses as we forgive those who trespass against us."

Hence, the feeling that people owe us something or the pain we experience is due to the evil deeds which others caused against us, etc., are obstacles for all internal progress of the soul.

Jesus the great Kabir said:

> *"Agree with thine adversary quickly,*
> *while thou art in the way with*
> *him; lest at any time the adversary*
> *deliver thee to the judge, and the*
> *judge deliver thee to the officer,*
> *and thou be cast into prison. Verily*

I say unto thee, Thou shalt by no
means come out thence, till thou
hast paid the uttermost farthing."
—Christian Bible, Matthew 5:25-26

If they owe us, we owe. If we demand to be repaid to the last denarius, we should first pay the last farthing.

This is the "law of the talion," "An eye for an eye and a tooth for a tooth," an absurd "vicious circle."

The apologies, compliance and the humiliations which we demand from others for the wrongs they caused us are also demanded from us, even if we consider ourselves to be "humble sheep."

So, to place oneself under unnecessary laws is an absurdity. It is better to place oneself under new influences.

The law of mercy is a more elevated influence than the law of the violent man, "An eye for an eye, a tooth for a tooth."

It is urgent, indispensable and non-excludable to place ourselves intelligently under the marvelous influences of the Gnostic esoteric work, in order to forget that people owe us and to eliminate from our psyche any form of self-consideration.

We must never allow within ourselves feelings of the wrongs inflicted on us, sentiments of revenge, resentment, negative emotions, anxieties, violence, envy, incessant remembering of debts, etc.

Gnosis is destined for those sincere aspirants who truly want to work and change.

If we observe people we can see in a direct way that each person has his own song.

Each one sings his own psychological song. I want to emphatically refer to the subject matter of "psychological accounting," which is the feeling that "people owe us." One complains, one auto-considers his own "self," etc.

Sometimes people "sing their song, just like that," without anyone winding them up, without anyone's invitation and on other occasions, after a few glasses of wine...

We affirm that our boring song must be eliminated, because it incapacitates us internally; it robs us of much energy.

In matters of revolutionary psychology, someone who sings too well (we are not referring to a beautiful voice or to physical singing) certainly cannot go beyond himself. He remains in the past...

A person impeded by sad songs cannot change his Level of Being. He cannot go beyond what he is.

In order to pass to a superior Level of Being, it is necessary to cease being what one is. We need to not be what we are.

If we continue being what we are, we will never pass to a superior Level of Being.

In the field of practical life, unusual things happen. Very often, a person starts a friendship with another, just because it is easy to sing his song to that person.

Unfortunately, such types of relationships end when the singer is asked to shut up, to change the record, to talk about something else, etc.

Then the resentful singer leaves in search of a new friend, of someone who is willing to listen to him for an indefinite time.

The singer demands comprehension, someone who comprehends him, as if it was easy to comprehend another person.

In order to comprehend another person, first of all, it is necessary to comprehend our own self. Unfortunately, the good singer believes that he comprehends himself.

Many are the disenchanted singers who sing the song of not being comprehended and dream with a marvelous world where they are the central figures.

Nevertheless, not all singers are public singers. There are also the reserved ones. They do not sing their song directly, but they do so secretly.

They are people who have worked much, who have suffered a great deal, who feel cheated. They think that life owes them all that which they were never capable of achieving.

Usually, they feel an internal sadness, a sensation of monotony and frightening boredom, inner exhaustion or frustration around which thoughts accumulate.

Unquestionably, secret songs prevent us from accessing the path of the realization of the Innermost Being.

Unfortunately, such inner secret songs go by unnoticed within ourselves, unless we intentionally observe them.

Obviously, all self-observation allows light to penetrate into ourselves within our inner depths.

No interior change can occur in our psyche unless we allow the light of self-observation to penetrate.

It is indispensable to observe oneself when alone in the same manner as when associated with people.

Very different "I's," very different thoughts, negative emotions, etc. present themselves when one is alone.

One is not always in good company when alone. It is just normal, very natural to be very badly accompanied when in complete solitude. The most negative and dangerous "I's" present themselves when one is alone.

If we want to transform ourselves radically, we need to sacrifice our own sufferings. Often we express our sufferings in articulated or inarticulated songs.

Chapter 25

Return and Recurrence

A person is what their life is. Therefore, if they do not modify anything within themselves, if they do not radically transform their life, if they do not work on themselves, they are miserably wasting their time.

Death is the return to the very beginning of one's life with the possibility of repeating it once again.

Much has been stated in pseudo-esoteric and pseudo-occultist literature about the subject of successive lives. Yet, it is better to be concerned about successive existences.

The life of each one of us, with all its seasons, is always the same. Life repeats itself from existence to existence throughout innumerable centuries.

Unquestionably, we continue in the seed of our descendants. This is something which has already been demonstrated.

The life of each one of us is individual. Life is a living movie that we carry along with us to eternity when we die.

Each one of us takes our movie with us and brings it back to project it once again on the screen of a new existence.

The repetition of dramas, comedies, and tragedies is a fundamental axiom of the law of recurrence.

The same circumstances always repeat themselves in each new existence. The actors of such scenes, which are always repeated, are those people who live in our interior, our "I's."

If we disintegrate those actors, those "I's" who originate the ever-repeating scenes of our lives, then the repetition of such circumstances would become more than impossible. Obviously, there cannot be any scenes without actors. This is irrefutable, indisputable.

This is how we can liberate ourselves from the laws of return and recurrence. This is how we can truly free ourselves.

Obviously, each of the characters ("I's") that we carry in our interior repeats, existence after existence, its same role. Therefore, if we disintegrate that "I," if the actor dies, the role concludes.

By reflecting seriously through inner self-observation on this subject matter, we discover the secret springs of the law of

recurrence or repetition of scenes in each
return.

If in the past existence at twenty-five
years of age a man had a love affair, it is
indubitable that in his new existence, the
"I" of taht commitment will seek the lady
of his dreams at the age of twenty-five
again.

If the lady in question was only fifteen
years old then, in her new existence, the
"I" of that affair will seek her beloved one
at the exact age again.

It is easy to comprehend that the two
"I's," both his and hers, seek each other
telepathically and meet once again in
order to repeat the love affair of their former existence.

Two enemies who fought to death in
a past existence will look for each other
again in the new existence to repeat their
tragedy at the corresponding age.

If in the past existence two persons
had a fight over real estate at the age
of forty years, they will find each other
telepathically at the same age in order to
repeat the same thing.

Thus, inside each one of us live many
people full of commitments. This is irrefutable.

A thief carries a "den" of thieves in themselves, each with different criminal commitments. A murderer carries within himself a "club" of murderers, and the lustful one carries a "whorehouse" in their psyche.

The critical thing about this subject matter is that the intellect ignores the existence of such people or "I's" within ourselves and of such commitments that are fatally fulfilled.

All those commitments of the "I's" which abide within us are happening regardless of our reasoning. These are commitments that we ignore, things that happen to us, events that are processed in the subconsciousness and unconsciousness.

This is why we have been rightfully told that everything happens to us just as when it rains and thunders.

Indeed, we have the illusion of doing; yet, we do nothing. Things happen to us. This is fatal, mechanical...

Our personality is merely the instrument of different people, "I's." Each one of those persons ("I's") fulfills its commitments through the personality.

Many things happen underneath our cognitive capacity. Unfortunately, we ignore what happens underneath our wretched reasoning.

We believe that we are wise, when indeed we do not even know that we do not know. We are miserable logs dragged by the boisterous waves of the sea of existence.

To emerge from within this misfortune, from within this unconsciousness, from within such an unfortunate state in which we find ourselves, is only possible by dying within ourselves...

How could we awaken without first dying? What is new arrives only with death! If the seed does not die, the plant does not sprout.

Those who truly awaken attain, as an outcome, full objectivity of the consciousness, authentic enlightenment, happiness.

"Newly born children are marvelous.
They enjoy total Self-cognizance.
They are totally awake."

Chapter 26
Infant's Self-cognizance

We have been wisely told that we have ninety-seven percent of subconsciousness and three percent of consciousness.

Plainly and bluntly speaking, we shall state that ninety-seven percent of the Essence that we carry within ourselves is bottled up, stuffed, inserted within each one of the "I's," which in their conjunction constitute the "myself."

Obviously, the Essence, or consciousness, bottled up within each "I," processes itself in accordance to its condition.

A determined percentage of consciousness is liberated when any "I" is disintegrated. Hence, the emancipation or liberation of the Essence or consciousness without the disintegration of each "I" is impossible.

The greater the quantity of disintegrated "I's," the greater the degree of Self-cognizance. The lesser the quantity of disintegrated "I's," the lesser the percentage of awakened consciousness.

Therefore, the awakening of consciousness is only possible by dissolving the "I," by dying in oneself, here and now.

Unquestionably, as long as the Essence or consciousness continues bottled up within each one of the "I's" that we carry within our interior, it will always be asleep, in a subconscious state.

It is urgent to transform the subconsciousness into consciousness. This is only possible by annihilating the "I's," by dying within ourselves.

So, it is impossible to awaken without first having died within ourselves.

Those who try to awaken first and then die do not possess a real experience of what they affirm. They advance resolutely on the path of error.

Newly born children are marvelous. They enjoy total self-cognizance. They are totally awake.

The Essence or consciousness is re-embodied within the body of the newly born child. This is what gives the baby its beauty.

We do not mean to state that one hundred percent of the Essence or consciousness is re-embodied within the newly born child; it is only the three percent of free consciousness that normally is not bottled up within the "I's."

Nevertheless, that free percentage of Essence, re-embodied within the organisms of newly born babies, gives them full self-cognizance, lucidity, etc.

Adults look at the newborn with a type of pity. They think that the baby is incognizant; nonetheless, they are lamentably mistaken.

The newborn looks at the adults exactly as they actually are: unconscious, cruel, perverse, etc.

The "I's" of the newborn come and go. They circle around the cradle and wish to enter into the new body. However, because the newborn child has not yet built a personality, all attempts by the "I's" to enter the new body are more than impossible.

Sometimes, babies are frightened when they see those phantoms or "I's" that approach their crib and then they cry, scream. Yet, adults do not understand and assume that the child is ill or is hungry or thirsty; such is the unconsciousness of adults.

As the new personality forms, the "I's" that come from previous existences penetrate the new body little by little.

When the totality of the "I's" have entered into the new body, then we appear in the world with that horrible ugliness that characterizes all of us. We then wander like somnambulists everywhere, always unconscious, always perverse.

When we die, three things go to the sepulcher:

1) The physical body

2) The organic vital body

3) The personality

The vital organic body floats like a phantom in front of the grave and disintegrates little by little, as the physical body also disintegrates.

The personality is subconscious or infraconscious. The personality enters and leaves the sepulcher whenever it wants. The personality rejoices when mourners bring flowers, it loves its relatives and dissolves very slowly until it becomes cosmic dust.

That which continues beyond the sepulcher is the ego, the pluralized "I," the myself, a bunch of devils, in which the Essence, the consciousness, is bottled up.

The ego, in its due time, returns and rein-corporates.

It is lamentable that the "I's" also re-embody when the new personality of the child is built.

ENGRAVING BY JOHAN VON CAROLSFELD.

"To begin to realize our own nothingness
and the misery in which we find ourselves
is absolutely impossible as long as that
concept of "more" exists in us."

Chapter 27
The Publican and
the Pharisee

When reflecting a little about the diverse circumstances of life, it is worthwhile to seriously comprehend the foundations we depend upon.

One person depends upon his position, another on money, a different one on his prestige, that other person on his past, someone else on this or that particular academic degree, etc.

The most curious thing about this matter is that all of us, whether rich or poor, need everybody else and live off everybody else, even if we are filled with pride and vanity.

Let us think for a moment on what could be taken away from us. What would our fate be in a revolution of blood and liquor? What would be left of the foundations that we depend upon? Woe to us! We believe ourselves to be very strong, yet we are horribly weak!

The "I" that in itself feels to be the foundation that we depend upon must be dissolved if indeed we wish for authentic bliss. That "I" underestimates people, feels it is better than the whole world, more perfect in everything, wealthier, more intelligent, more experienced in life, etc.

It is very opportune to quote the parable of Jesus the great Kabir, about the two men who went up into the temple to pray. He spoke this parable to those who felt secure in their self-righteousness and who despised others. Jesus the Christ stated:

> *"Two men went up into the temple to pray; the one a Pharisee, and the other a Publican. The Pharisee stood and prayed thus with himself, 'God, I thank thee, that I am not as other men are, extortioners, unjust, adulterers, or even as this Publican. I fast twice in the week, I give tithes of all that I possess.' And the Publican standing afar off, would not lift up so much as his eyes unto heaven, but smote upon his breast, saying, 'God be merciful to me, a sinner.' I tell you, this man went down to his house justified rather than the other: for every one that exalteth himself shall be abased; and he that*

humbleth himself shall be exalted."
—Christian Bible, Luke 18: 10-14

To begin to realize our own nothingness and the misery in which we find ourselves is absolutely impossible as long as
that concept of "more" exists in us.

Examples: I am more just than that
one, wiser than that fellow, more virtuous
than the other fellow, richer, more experienced in the things of life, more chaste,
more responsible in my duties, etc.

It is not possible to go through the
eye of a needle as long as we are "rich,"
as long as that complex of "more" exists
within us.

> *"It is easier for a camel to go through
> the eye of a needle, than for a rich
> man to enter into the kingdom of
> God."* —Christian Bible, Matthew 19:24

The feeling that "my school is the best
and my neighbor's school is worthless";
that "my religion is the only authentic one and that all others religions are
false and perverse"; that "such a fellow's
spouse is a lousy spouse and that mine
is a saint"; that "my friend Robert is a
drunkard, yet I am wise and abstemious,
etc.," is what makes us feel rich. That is

the reason why we are all the "camels" of the biblical parable in relation to the esoteric work.

It is urgent to observe ourselves from moment to moment with the purpose of clearly knowing the foundations we depend upon.

When we discover that which offends us the most at any given moment, when someone bothers us by dint of one thing or another, we then discover the foundations we psychologically depend upon.

Such foundations constitute, according to the Christian Gospel, "the sands upon which we built our house."

It is necessary to carefully notice when and how much one despises others, perhaps one feels to be superior because one's academic degree or one's social position, or because of one's acquired experience or money, etc.

It is terrible to feel oneself rich, to feel superior to this or that fellow because of this reason or another. People like this cannot enter into the Kingdom of Heaven.

It is worthwhile to discover what flatters us, what satisfies our vanity. This will show us the foundations we depend upon.

Nevertheless, such a type of observation must not be something merely theoretical. We must be practical and observe ourselves closely in a direct way from instant to instant.

When one begins to comprehend his own misery and nothingness, when one abandons the delirium of grandeur, when one discovers the foolishness of so many academic degrees, honors and vain superiorities over our fellowmen, then it is an unmistakable sign that one is beginning to change.

If one clings to that which says, "my house," "my money," "my properties," "my job," "my virtues," "my intellectual capacities," "my artistic capacities," "my knowledge," "my prestige," etc., then one cannot change.

So, clinging to "mine" or to "my" is more than enough in order to prevent recognition of our nothingness and interior misery.

One is astonished in front of the spectacle of a fire or a shipwreck. At such a moment desperate people often seize many things that are ludicrous, things of no importance.

Wretched people! They feel themselves in those objects; they lean on silly objects; they become attached to objects which do not have the least bit of importance.

To feel that one exists through external things, and to lay our foundations upon those things is equivalent to being in a state of total unconsciousness.

The sentiment of the "Seity" (the real Being) is only possible by dissolving all those "I's" which we carry within our interior. Before this annihilation, such a sentiment becomes more than impossible.

Unfortunately, the adorers of the "I" do not accept this. They believe themselves to be gods. They believe that they already possess those "glorious bodies" that Paul of Tarsus spoke about. They assume that the "I" is divine. Nobody can erase those absurdities from their minds.

One does not know what to do with such people. The doctrine is explained to them, yet they do not understand it. They always hold fast to the sands upon which they built their house. They are always engrossed within their dogmas, within their whims, within their foolishness.

If those people were to observe themselves seriously, they would then verify
by themselves the Doctrine of the Many.
They would discover within themselves all
the multiplicity of persons or "I's" which
live within our interior.

How can the real feeling of our true
Being be experienced within ourselves,
when instead, those "I's" are feeling for us
and thinking for us?

The most critical part of all this tragedy is that we think that we are thinking,
that we feel that we are feeling, when,
indeed it is someone else who in a given
moment thinks through our tormented
mind and feels through our afflicted
heart.

Oh, how wretched we are, how many
times do we believe we are loving, when
what is happening is that another person
filled with lust is utilizing the heart center.

How wretched we are; we confuse animal passion for love! Nevertheless, it is
someone else within ourselves, within our
personality, who goes through these con-
fusions.

All of us think that we will never pro-
nounce those words of the Pharisee in the

biblical parable, "God, I thank thee that I am not as other men are," etc.

Nevertheless, and even if this might appear incredible, this is the way we behave daily. The butcher in the market says, "I am not like the rest of the butchers that sell bad quality meat and exploit people."

The vendor of textiles in the store exclaims, "I am not like the rest of the merchants that know how to steal when measuring and who have grown rich."

The milk vendor affirms, "I am not like the rest of the milk vendors that put water in their milk. I like to be honest."

The mistress of the house comments to her visitor the following, "I am not like such a lady who flirts with other men. I am, thanks to God, a decent person, since I am faithful to my husband."

Conclusion: Others are scoundrels, unjust, adulterers, thieves and perverse persons; yet each one of us is a humble lamb, "a saint with a golden halo," who is worthy to be shown as a golden masterpiece inside any temple.

How foolish we are! We often think that we never do all the foolishness and perversities that we see others do; this is why we arrive at the conclusion that we are magnificent persons. Unfortunately, we do not see the foolishness and wretched things we do.

There are unusual moments in life when our mind rests without worries of any kind, when the mind is calm, when the mind is in silence. Then, the new arrives. In such instants, it is possible to see the bases, the foundations we depend upon.

When the mind is in profound interior restfulness, we can verify for ourselves the crude reality of the sand of life, upon which we built our house. (Read Matthew 7, Verses 24-29; the parable that talks about the two foundations).

MOSES, A SYMBOL OF CONSCIOUS WILLPOWER. ENGRAVING BY GUSTAVE DORÉ

"Whosoever truly possesses free willpower
can originate new circumstances. Whosoever
has his willpower bottled up in the pluralized
"I" is a victim of circumstances."

Chapter 28

Willpower

The "Great Work" is, first of all, the creation of the true human being by dint of our will, based on conscious labors and voluntary sufferings.

The "Great Work" is the inner conquest of oneself, of our true liberty in God.

Therefore, if in reality we want the perfect emancipation of our willpower, we need, with a maximum and unavoidable urgency, to disintegrate all those "I's" that live in our interior.

Nicholas Flammel and Raymond Lully were both meager men, yet they liberated their will and accomplished innumerable psychological prodigies that caused astonishment.

Agrippa never progressed past the first part of the "Great Work." He lamentably died while struggling in the disintegration of his "I's," with the objective of possessing himself and establishing his independence.

The perfect emancipation of willpower assures the sage absolute dominion over fire, air, water, and earth.

The assertion of our former paragraphs, in relation with the sovereign might of the emancipated willpower, may seem exaggerated to many students of contemporary psychology. Nonetheless, the Bible narrates wonders about Moses.

According to Philo, Moses was an initiate in the lands of the Pharaohs on the banks of the river Nile. He was a priest of Osiris, and he was the Pharaoh's cousin, educated among the columns of Isis, the Divine Mother, and of Osiris, our Father who is in secret.

Moses was a descendant of the Patriarch Abraham, the great Chaldean Magus, and of the very respectable Isaac.

Moses, the man who liberated the electric might of the willpower, possesses the gift of prodigies. This is known by the divine ones and humans. So it is written.

All that the sacred scriptures state about this Hebrew leader is certainly extraordinary, portentous.

Moses transformed his staff into a serpent. He transformed one of his hands into that of a leper and then restored it to health again.

His power was clearly demonstrated in the "burning bush;" thus, people comprehended, knelt and prostrated themselves.

Moses handled a magical wand, emblem of royal power, of the priestly power of the initiate in the great mysteries of life and death.

In front of the Pharaoh, Moses changed the water of the Nile into blood; the fish died, the sacred river became infected, the Egyptians could not drink from it, and the irrigation canals of the Egyptians poured out blood onto the fields.

Moses did more; he succeeded in causing millions of disproportionate, gigantic and monstrous frogs to appear out of the river and swarm through the houses. Then, upon his signal (an indication of a free and sovereign willpower) those horrible frogs disappeared.

However, since the Pharaoh did not set the Israelites free, Moses worked new miracles: he covered the earth with filth, stirred up clouds of repugnant and filthy flies, which he later gave himself the luxury of driving away.

He unchained the frightening plague and all the flocks died, except those of the Jews.

He took ashes from the furnace, state the sacred scriptures, threw them into the air and they fell on the Egyptians, causing them pustules and boils.

Putting forth his famous magical wand, Moses caused a hailstorm from heaven which mercilessly destroyed and killed. Next, he caused the fiery lightning bolt to strike. The terrifying thunder roared and it rained horribly. Then, with a signal, everything returned to calm.

However, the Pharaoh continued to be inflexible. Moses, with a tremendous strike of his magical wand, as if by magic, caused clouds of locusts to appear. Then darkness came. Another strike of the wand and all returned to its original order.

The end of that Biblical drama of the Old Testament is very well known: Jehovah intervened, causing the firstborn of the Egyptians to die, and the Pharaoh had no other choice but to let the Hebrews leave.

Next, Moses made use of his magical wand to separate the waters of the Red Sea and to cross it with dry feet.

When the Egyptian soldiers threw themselves in pursuit of the Israelites, Moses, with a signal, caused the waters to close again, swallowing the followers.

Unquestionably, on reading this, many pseudo-occultists wish they could do the same, and have the same powers of Moses. However, this is more than impossible as long as the willpower continues to be bottled up in each and every one of those "I's" which we carry within the different depths of our psyche.

The Essence, engrossed in the "myself," is the Genie of Aladdin's lamp, wishing for liberty... Once the Genie is free, he can accomplish miracles.

The Essence is "conscience-willpower," unfortunately processing itself in virtue of our own conditioning.

When our willpower is liberated, then it blends or fuses itself with the universal willpower. Thus, as an outcome of this, when integrated like this, our willpower becomes sovereign.

The individual willpower fused with the universal willpower can accomplish all the miracles of Moses.

There are three types of action:

1. Those which correspond to the law of accidents.

2. Those which belong to the law of recurrence, actions always repeated in each existence.

3. Actions which are intentionally determined by the conscious willpower.

Unquestionably, only persons who have liberated their willpower through the death of the "myself" shall be able to accomplish new acts born from their free willpower.

The common and current acts of mankind are always either the result of the law of recurrence or the mere product of mechanical accidents.

Whosoever truly possesses free willpower can originate new circumstances.

Whosoever has their willpower bottled up in the pluralized "I" is a victim of circumstances.

In all the Biblical pages, there is a marvelous display of high magic, seership, prophesy, miracles, transfigurations, and the resurrection of the dead by insufflation or laying of hands, or by a fixed look upon the root of the nose, etc.

Abounding in the Bible is massage, holy oil, magnetic passes, the application of a little saliva on the sick part of the body, reading another person's thoughts, transportations, apparitions, words coming from heaven, etc., true marvels of the liberated, emancipated and sovereign conscious willpower.

Witches? Sorcerers? Black magicians? They are found everywhere like wild weeds. They are, however, not saints nor prophets, nor adepts of the White Fraternity.

No one can arrive at "real illumination" nor exercise the absolute priesthood of conscious willpower, if they have not first died radically in themselves here and now.

Many people write us frequently complaining of not possessing illumination, asking for powers, demanding clues that shall convert them into magicians, etc., but they never become interested in observing and knowing themselves, or in disintegrating those psychic aggregates, those "I's" within which the willpower, the Essence, is absorbed.

Persons like that are obviously condemned to failure. They are people who covet the faculties of the saints but who have in no way decided to die in themselves.

The elimination of errors is something magical, marvelous by itself, which implies rigorous psychological self-observation.

The exercise of powers is possible when the marvelous power of the will is radically liberated.

Unfortunately, since the willpower of people is absorbed in each "I," obviously their willpower is divided into multiple wills that process themselves in virtue of their own conditioning.

It is clear to comprehend that each "I" possesses its own particular, unconscious will.

The innumerable wills engrossed in the "I's" frequently clash with each other, making them impotent, weak, miserable, victims of circumstances, incapable, due to that reason.

Chapter 29

Decapitation

As one works on oneself, one comprehends more and more the necessity
of radically eliminating from one's inner
nature all that which makes us so abominable.

The worst circumstances of life, the
most critical situations, and the most difficult deeds are always marvelous for intimate self-discovery.

The most secret "I's" always sur-
face in those unsuspected, critical
moments, and when we least expect them.
Unquestionably, if we are alert, we discover ourselves.

The most tranquil moments of life are
precisely the least favorable for the work
upon oneself.

There are moments in life that are too
complicated. In those moments we have
the marked tendency of identifying easily
with the events and completely forgetting
about ourselves. In those instances, we do
foolish things which lead nowhere. If, in
those moments, we are alert, if instead of
losing our minds we remember our own

selves, we then would discover with astonishment certain "I's" whose possibility of existence we never suspected in the least.

The sense of intimate self-observation is atrophied in every human being. Yet, such a sense will develop in a progressive manner by working seriously, by observing oneself from moment to moment.

Thus, as the sense of self-observation gradually develops through its continuous use, we shall become more capable each time of directly perceiving those "I's" whose existence we previously never had the least bit of data about.

Indeed, while in the sight of the sense of inner self-observation, each of those "I's" which inhabit our interior assume this or that figure. This figure is secretly related to the defect that is personified within it. Undoubtedly, the image of each of those "I's" has a certain unmistakable psychological flavor. We, through this image, instinctively apprehend, capture, trap its inner nature, and the defect which characterizes it.

In the beginning, the esotericist does not know where to start. We feel the necessity of working on ourselves but are completely disoriented.

Yet, if we take advantage of the critical moments, of the more unpleasant situations, the most adverse instances, we shall then discover, if we are alert, our outstanding defects, the "I's" that we must urgently disintegrate.

Sometimes one can begin with anger or pride or with the wretched moment of lust, etc..

However, if we truly want a definite change, it is necessary to take note of our daily psychological states.

Before going to bed, it is wise to examine the events that occurred during the day, the embarrassing situations, the thunderous laughter of Aristophanes, or the subtle smile of Socrates.

It is possible that we may have hurt someone with a laugh, or that we caused someone to fall ill with a smile or with a look that was out of place.

Let us remember that in pure esotericism good is all that is in its place; bad is all that is out of its place. For instance, water is good in its place, but if the water is out of place, if it floods the house, then it would cause damage; it would be bad and harmful.

Likewise, fire in the kitchen, when in its place, besides being useful, is good. Yet, the fire out of its place, burning the furniture of the living room, would be bad and harmful.

Thus, any virtue, no matter how holy it might be, is good in its place; yet, it is bad and harmful out of its place. We can harm others with our virtues. Therefore, it is indispensable to place virtues in their corresponding place.

What would you say about a priest who preaches the Word of the Lord inside a brothel? What would you say about a meek and tolerant male who blesses a gang of assailants attempting to rape his wife and daughters? What would you say about that type of tolerance taken to such an extreme? What would you say about the charitable attitude of a man who, instead of taking food home, shares his money among beggars who have a vice? What would be your opinion of a helpful man who in a given moment lends a dagger to a murderer?

Remember, dear reader, that crime also hides within the rhythm of poetry.

There is much virtue in the perverse one and as much evil in the virtuous one.

Even though it may appear incredible, crime also hides in the very perfume of prayer.

Crime disguises itself as a saint. It uses the best virtues; it presents itself as a martyr and even officiates in the sacred temples.

As the sense of intimate self-observation develops in us, through its continuous use we can see all those "I's" that serve as a basic foundation to our individual temperament, whether it be sanguine or nervous, phlegmatic or bilious.

Although you may not believe it, dear reader, the fact is that behind the temperament that we possess, within the most remote profundities of our psyche, the most abominable diabolic creations are hidden.

To see such creations, to observe these monstrosities of hell within which our very same consciousness is imprisoned, is only possible with the ever progressive development of the sense of intimate self-observation.

Therefore, as long as a human being has not dissolved these creations of hell, these aberrations of ourselves, undoubtedly in the deepest part, in the most pro-

found part of ourselves, we will continue
being something that must not exist, a
deformity, an abomination.

The most critical aspect of all of this
is that the abominable person does not
become aware of our own abomination.
We believe ourselves to be beautiful, just,
a good person, and we even complain that
others do not understand us. We lament
the ingratitude of our fellowmen. We say
that they do not understand us. We cry,
affirming that they owe us, that they have
paid us back with black coins, etc.

The sense of intimate self-observation
allows us to verify for ourselves, and in a
direct manner, the secret work by which
in a given time we are dissolving this or
that "I" (this or that psychological defect),
possibly discovered in difficult conditions
and when we least suspect it.

Have you, sometime in your life, ever
thought of what you like or dislike the
most? Have you reflected on the secret
causes of action? Why do you want to
have a beautiful house? Why do you
desire the latest model car? Why do
you want to always be wearing the latest fashion? Why do you covet not being
covetous? What offended you the most

in a given moment? What flattered you the most yesterday? Why do you feel superior to this or that fellow in a specific moment? At what hour did you feel superior to someone? Why do you feel conceited when you relate your triumphs? Couldn't you keep quiet when they gossiped about someone you know? Did you receive the goblet of liquor out of courtesy? Did you accept smoking, although not having the vice, possibly because of the concept of education or out of manliness? Are you sure that you were sincere in your chatter? And when you justify yourself, when you praise yourself, when you boast about your triumphs and do so repeating what you have previously told others, do you comprehend that you are vain?

The sense of intimate self-observation, in addition to allowing you to see clearly the "I" that you are dissolving, will also allow you to see the pathetic and defined results of your internal Work.

In the beginning, these creations of hell, these psychic aberrations that unfortunately characterize you, are more ugly and monstrous than the most horrendous beasts that exist at the bottom of the oceans or in the most profound jungles of the earth. Yet, as you advance in your work, you will be able to evince through the sense of internal self-observation the outstanding fact that those abominations lose bulk; they grow smaller.

It is intriguing to know that such bestialities, as they decrease in size, as they lose bulk and become smaller, they gain in beauty; they slowly assume a childlike figure. Finally, they disintegrate; they become a cloud of cosmic dust. Then the imprisoned Essence is liberated; it is emancipated; it awakens.

Undoubtedly, the mind cannot fundamentally alter any psychological defect.

Obviously the intellect can give itself the luxury of naming a defect with this or that name, of justifying it, or passing it from one level to another, etc. But it could not by itself annihilate it, disintegrate it.

We urgently need a flaming power superior to the mind, a power that by itself is capable of reducing this or that psychological defect to a mere cloud of cosmic dust.

Fortunately there exists in us that marvelous fire that the ancient medieval

alchemists baptized with the mysterious
name of Stella Maris, the Virgin of the
Sea, the Azoth of the science of Hermes,
Tonantzin of Aztec Mexico, that derivative from our own intimate Being, God-
Mother within our interior, who is always
symbolized with the sacred serpent of the
great mysteries.

If after having observed and profound-
ly comprehended this or that psychological defect (this or that "I"), we beg our
individual Cosmic Mother, since each of
us has his own, to disintegrate, to reduce
to a cloud of cosmic dust, this or that
defect, that is, the "I," the motive of our
interior work. Then you can be sure that
it will lose mass and it will be slowly pul-
verized.

All of this naturally implies successive
deep works, always continuous, since no
"I" can ever be disintegrated instantly.
The sense of intimate self-observation will
be able to see the progressive advance of
the work in relation with the abomination whose disintegration truly interests
us.

Although it may appear incredible,
Stella Maris is the astral signature of the
human sexual potency.

Obviously, Stella Maris has the effective power to disintegrate the aberrations that we carry in our psychological interior.

The decapitation of John the Baptist is something that invites us to reflect.

No radical psychological change is possible if we do not first pass through decapitation.

Our own derivative-Being, Tonantzin, Stella Maris, as an electric power, is unknown to the entire humanity. Yet, she abides latent in the depth of our psyche. Clearly, she enjoys the power that permits her to decapitate any "I" before its final disintegration.

Stella Maris is that philosophical fire that is found latent in all organic and inorganic matter.

Psychological impulses can provoke the intensive action of such a fire and then decapitation is made possible.

Some "I's" are usually decapitated at the beginning of the psychological work, others in the middle and the last ones at the end. Stella Maris, as a sexual igneous power, has full consciousness of the work that must be performed. She per-

forms the decapitation at the opportune
moment, at the appropriate instant.

As long as the disintegration of all
these psychological abominations, of all
this lasciviousness, of all these curses:
robbery, envy, secret or manifest adultery,
ambition for money or psychic powers,
etc. has not been produced, even when we
think ourselves honorable persons, true
to our word, sincere, courteous, charitable, beautiful in our interior, etc., obviously we are nothing more than whitened
sepulchers, beautiful from outside, yet
full of disgusting filthiness inside.

Erudition is good for nothing: the
pseudo-wisdom of the complete information on the sacred writings, whether these
be from the east or the west, from the
north or the south, the pseudo-occultism,
the pseudo-esotericism, the absolute
certainty that one is well informed, the
intransigent sectarianism with complete
convincing, etc. This is because, indeed, at
the bottom exists what we ignore, which
are: creations of hell, curses, monstrosities
that hide behind the pretty face, behind
the venerable countenance, underneath
the most holy garb of the sacred leader,
etc.

We have to be sincere with ourselves and ask ourselves what we want, if we have come to the Gnostic teaching out of mere curiosity. If in reality what we desire is not to pass through decapitation, then we are fooling ourselves; we are defending our own filthiness; we are proceeding hypocritically.

In the most venerable schools of esoteric wisdom and esotericism there are many sincerely mistaken ones who truly want to Self-realize, yet they are not dedicated to the disintegration of their interior abominations.

Numerous are these people who assume that through good intentions it is possible to attain sanctity. Obviously, as long as one does not work intensely on those "I's" that we carry within our interior, they will continue to exist beneath the depth of our godly appearance and our upright conduct.

The time has come for us to know that we are perverse ones disguised with the robe of sanctity: wolves in sheepskin, cannibals dressed in formal clothing, executioners hidden behind the sacred sign of the cross, etc.

As majestic as we may seem inside our temples or inside our classrooms of light and harmony, as serene and sweet as we may seem to our fellowmen, as reverent and humble as we may appear, the abominations of hell and all the monstrosities of the wars continue to exist at the bottom of our psyche.

In revolutionary psychology, the necessity of a radical transformation is evident to us and this is only possible by declaring on oneself a merciless and cruel war to the death.

Indeed, all of us are worthless, each one of us is the disgrace, the abomination of the earth.

Fortunately, John the Baptist taught us the secret way: to die in oneself through psychological decapitation.

THE MARTYRDOM OF JOHN, A SYMBOL OF MYSTICAL DEATH

"In revolutionary psychology, the necessity of
a radical transformation is evident to us and
this is only possible by declaring on oneself
a merciless and cruel war to the death."

Chapter 30

The Permanent Center of Gravity

It is impossible to have continuity of purpose without a true individuality.

Therefore, if the psychological individual does not exist, if many persons live within each one of us, if there is no responsible person within, it would be an absurdity to demand continuity of purpose from someone.

We know well that many persons live within a person. Hence, the full sense of responsibility does not really exist in us.

We cannot take seriously what any particular "I" affirms at any given moment because of the concrete fact that any other "I" can affirm exactly the opposite at any other moment.

What is critical of all this subject matter is that many people believe that they possess a sense of moral responsibility, yet they deceive themselves when affirming that they are always the same.

There are people who at some moment of their existence come to the Gnostic studies: they glow through the force of their enthusiasm; they become devoted to the esoteric work and even swear to consecrate the whole of their existence to these matters.

Unquestionably, all the brothers and sisters of our movement even admire such an enthusiastic one. One cannot but feel great happiness in listening to these kinds of people, so devoted and definitely sincere.

However, the idyll does not last very long. Any given day, due to this or that reason, just or unjust, simple or complex, the person withdraws from Gnosis and abandons the work. Thus, in order to right the wrong, or in trying to justify himself, he joins any other mystical organization and thinks that he is then doing better.

All this coming and going, all this incessant change of schools, sects, religions, is due to the multiplicity of "I's" that struggle amongst themselves for their own supremacy within our interior.

This constant fluttering around among organizations, from idea to idea, this change of opinions is but normal, since every "I" possesses its own criteria, its own mind, its own ideas.

Therefore, such a person in himself is nothing more than a machine who just easily serves as a vehicle to one "I" or another.

Some mystical "I's" deceive themselves after having abandoned this sect or the other. They decide to believe themselves to be gods. Thus, they shine like fatuous lights and finally disappear.

There are people who show themselves for a moment to the esoteric work, then, all of a sudden, another "I" intervenes. Thus, they definitely abandon these studies and allow themselves to be swallowed by life.

Obviously, if one does not struggle against life, then one is devoured by life. Very rare are the aspirants who truly do not allow themselves to be swallowed up by life.

The permanent center of gravity cannot exist within us as long as a whole multiplicity of "I's" exists inside of us.

It is normal that not all people achieve the realization of the Innermost Self.

We know very well that the realization of the Innermost Being demands continuity of purpose. Therefore, it is not strange that only very few people can attain the profound inner Self-realization, since it is very difficult to find someone with a permanent center of gravity.

What is normal in this subject matter is for someone to become enthusiastic for the esoteric work and then to abandon it. What is strange is for someone to not abandon the work and to reach the goal.

Indeed, in the name of the truth, we affirm that the Sun is conducting a very complex and terribly difficult laboratory experiment.

Germs (seeds) exist within the intellectual animal (mistakenly called the human being) that when conveniently developed can convert us into solar humans.

Nonetheless, it is not irrelevant to clarify that the development of these germs cannot be taken for granted. What is normal is for these germs to degenerate and become lamentably lost.

In any event, the above-mentioned germs which can convert us into solar humans need an adequate environment. It is well known that the seed in a sterile environment does not germinate; it is lost.

Continuity of purpose and a normal physical body are necessary in order for the real seed of the human being, deposited in our sexual glands, to be able to germinate.

Yet, if the scientists continue experimenting with the glands of internal secretion, then any possibility of development for these aforementioned germs can be lost.

Although it may seem incredible, the ants already passed through a similar process, in a remote, archaic past of our planet Earth.

One is filled with wonder when contemplating the perfection of the nests of ants. There is no doubt that the order established in any ants' nest is overwhelming.

The initiates who have awakened their consciousness know through direct mystical experience that in ages which the most famous historians of the world do not even remotely suspect, the ants were a human race who created a very powerful socialist civilization.

At that time, the dictators of such a race eliminated the diverse religious sects and free will, for all of these things undermined power away from them. They needed to be totalitarians in the most complete sense of the word.

So, in these conditions, after having eliminated individual initiative and religious rights, these intellectual animals precipitated themselves downwards into the path of devolution and degeneration.

Moreover, they added to the aforementioned scientific experiments: transplant of organs, glands, hormonal tests, etc., whose outcome was the gradual diminishing in size and the morphological alteration of their human organisms until finally, through the ages, they became the ants that we know now.

Thus, their entire civilization, all those movements related with their established social order, became mechanical and were inherited from parents to children. Today, one is astonished when seeing an ants' nest, yet we cannot but lament its lack of intelligence.

Therefore, if we do not work on ourselves, we devolve and degenerate horribly.

Indeed, the experiment that the Sun is conducting in the laboratory of Nature, besides being difficult, has given very few positive results.

The creation of solar humans is only possible when true cooperation exists within each one of us.

Thus, if first of all we do not establish a permanent center of gravity within our interior, then the creation of the solar human being is impossible.

How can we have continuity of purpose if we do not establish a center of gravity in our psyche?

Certainly, any race created by the Sun has no other objective in Nature but to serve the interests of this creation and the solar experiment.

Yet, if the Sun fails in its experiment, then it loses all interest in such a race. Thus, such a race is left condemned to destruction and devolution.

Each of the root races that have existed on the face of the Earth served the solar experiment. From each root race, the Sun has managed to get a few to fruition, that is to say the Sun has harvested small groups of solar humans.

After a root race has given its fruits, it disappears in a progressive manner, or perishes violently due to great catastrophes.

The creation of solar humans is possible when one struggles to become independent from the lunar forces. There is no doubt that all those "I's" that we carry within our psyche are exclusively of a lunar type.

By no means is it possible to liberate ourselves from the lunar force if we do not previously establish within ourselves a permanent center of gravity.

How can we dissolve the total of the pluralized "I" if we do not have a continuity of purpose? In what way can we have continuity of purpose without previously having established within our psyche a permanent center of gravity?

Hence, this contemporary race has condemned itself towards devolution and degeneration, since instead of becoming independent of the lunar influence it has unquestionably lost all interest for the solar intelligence.

It is not possible for the true human being to appear through the mechanics of evolution. We know very well that evolution and its twin sister devolution are nothing else but two laws which constitute the mechanical axis of all Nature. One evolves to a certain perfectly defined point, and then the devolving process follows. Every ascent is followed by a descent and vice-versa.

We are machines that are controlled exclusively by different "I's." We serve Nature's economy. We do not have a defined individuality as is erroneously supposed by many pseudo-esotericists and pseudo-occultists.

We need to change with maximum urgency so that the germs of the human being will give its fruits.

We can become solar humans only by working on ourselves with true continuity of purpose and a complete sense of moral responsibility. This implies the total consecration of our existence to the esoteric work on ourselves.

Those who hope to reach the solar state through the mechanics of evolution fool themselves and condemn themselves, in fact, to a devolving degeneration.

In the esoteric work, we cannot afford the luxury of versatility. Those who have fickle ideas, those who work on their psyche today and let themselves be swallowed by life tomorrow, those who seek subterfuges and justifications in order to abandon the esoteric work will degenerate and devolve.

Some postpone the error, leave everything for tomorrow while they improve their economic situation, without taking into consideration that the solar experiment is something very different from their personal criteria and their aforementioned projects.

It is not so easy to become a solar human when we carry the Moon in our interior (the ego is lunar).

The Earth has two moons. The second one is named Lilith and is a little farther away than the white moon.

Astronomers often see Lilith like a lentil, since it is very small in size. It is the black moon.

The most disastrous forces of the ego come to the Earth from Lilith and produce infrahuman and bestial psychological results.

The crimes mentioned in the news, the most monstrous murders in history, the most unsuspected crimes, etc. are due to the vibratory waves of Lilith.

These two lunar influences are represented within the human being through the ego that we carry in our interior and which makes of us true failures.

Therefore, if we do not see the urgency of surrendering our total existence to the work on ourselves with the purpose of liberating ourselves from the double lunar force, then we shall end up swallowed up by the Moon, devolving, degenerating more and more into certain states which we could very well classify as unconscious and infraconscious.

The sad part of all this is that we do not possess true individuality. If we had a permanent center of gravity we would then truly work seriously in order to achieve the solar state.

There are so many excuses in these matters, so many evasions, so many fascinating attractions, that it usually becomes almost impossible to comprehend the urgency of the esoteric work.

Nevertheless, the small amount that we have of free will and the Gnostic teaching oriented towards practical work can serve as a basis for our noble intentions in relation to the solar experiment.

What we are stating here is not understandable by the fickle mind. The fickle mind reads this chapter and then forgets it; it reads another book, then another. To that end, our fickle mind tends to end up joining any institution which sells us a passport to heaven, that talks to us in a more optimistic manner, that assures us of comforts in the beyond.

This is how people are mere marionettes controlled by invisible strings, mechanical dolls with fickle ideas and without continuity of purpose.

Chapter 31

The Gnostic
Esoteric Work

In order to work seriously on ourselves,
it is urgent to study Gnosis and to utilize
the practical ideas we give in this book.

Nonetheless, we cannot work on ourselves with the intention of dissolving
this or that "I," without having previously
observed it.

The observation of oneself permits a
ray of light to enter our interior.

Each "I" manifests itself one way
through the head, another way through
the heart, and in another way through the
sexual center.

We need to observe the "I" which we
have captured at a given moment; it is
urgent to see it in each of these three centers of our organism.

If we are alert and vigilant, like a
watchman in time of war, while relating
with other people, we can then discover
ourselves.

Do you recall when your vanity was
hurt by someone? Your pride? What

upset you the most during the day? Why did you have that vexation? What was its secret cause? Study this, observe your head, heart, and sexual center...

Practical life is a marvelous school. So, through interaction with others we can discover those "I's" that we carry within our interior.

Any annoyance, any incident can lead us through inner self-observation to the discovery of any "I," whether it be of self-esteem, envy, jealousy, anger, covetous-ness, suspicion, calumny, lust, etc.

We need to know ourselves before we can know others. It is urgent to learn to see others' point of view.

If we place ourselves in the place of others, we discover that the psychological defects that we attribute to others exist in abundance within our interior.

To love our neighbor is indispensable; however, in the esoteric work, if one does not firstly learn how to place his own self in the position of another person, one cannot love others.

Cruelty will continue to exist on the face of the Earth as long as we have not learned to put ourselves in the place of others.

But if we do not have the courage of seeing ourselves, then how can we put ourselves in the place of others?

Why should we only see the bad side of people?

The mechanical antipathy towards another person that we meet for the first time indicates that we do not know how to put ourselves in the place of our fellowmen. This indicates that we do not love our fellowmen, that we have our consciousness extremely asleep.

Do we feel antipathy towards a certain person? Why? Perhaps he drinks? Let us observe him... Are we certain of our virtue? Are we certain of not carrying the "I" of drunkenness within our interior?

When we see a drunkard doing all kinds of stupidities, it would be best if we said to ourselves, "This is me, what tomfoolery am I doing...?"

Are you an honest and virtuous woman and because of that you do not like a certain woman? Do you feel antipathy towards her? Why? Do you feel sure of yourself? Do you believe that you do not have the "I" of lust within your interior? Do you think that this woman, discredited by her scandals and lasciviousness, is perverse? Are you sure that the lasciviousness and perversity that you see in that woman does not exist within your interior? It would be better to observe yourself intimately, and while in profound meditation you may occupy the place of that woman you despise.

If indeed we yearn for a radical change, then it is urgent to value the Gnostic esoteric work. It is indispensable to comprehend and appreciate it.

It is indispensable to know how to love our fellowmen, to study Gnosis, and to take these teachings to all people. Otherwise, we will fall into egotism.

If we dedicate ourselves to the esoteric work on ourselves, but do not give these teachings to others, our inner progress becomes then very difficult due to lack of love for our fellow men.

> "For whosoever gives, to him shall be given, and the more he gives, the more he shall receive, but whosoever gives not, from him shall be taken away even what he has." —Christian Bible, Matthew 13:12, Mark 4:25

This is the law.

Chapter 32

Prayer in the Work

Observation, judgement, and execution are the three basic factors of dissolution.

First: one observes oneself.

Second: judgement is passed.

Third: execution takes place.

In war, spies are first observed; secondly, they are judged; thirdly, they are shot.

Self-discovery and self-revelation are in our interrelationships. Therefore, whosoever renounces living with his fellowmen also renounces self-discovery.

Any incident in life, regardless of how insignificant it may seem, undoubtedly has as its cause an intimate actor within us, a psychic aggregate, an "I."

Self-discovery is possible when we are in a state of alert perception, alert novelty.

Any "I" discovered flagrantly must be carefully observed in our mind, heart, and sexual center.

Any "I" of lust could manifest itself in the heart as love and in the mind as an ideal. Yet, as we pay attention to the sexual center, we may feel a certain morbid, unmistakable excitement.

The judgment of any "I" must be definitive. We need to sit it down on the bench of the accused and judge it mercilessly.

Evasion, justification, and consideration must be eliminated if in reality we want to be conscious of the "I" that we struggle to extirpate from our psyche.

Execution is different. It would not be possible to execute any "I" without previously observing it and judging it.

Prayer in the psychological work is fundamental for the dissolution of the "I." If indeed we want to disintegrate this or that "I," then we need a power superior to the mind.

The mind by itself can never disintegrate any "I"; this is indisputable and irrefutable.

To pray is to talk with God. If we truly want to disintegrate "I's," then we must appeal to God the Mother in the depths of our heart. Those who do not love their Mother, the ungrateful children, will fail in the work upon themselves.

Each of us has our particular, individual Divine Mother. She, in Herself, is a part of our own Being, but a derivative part.

All ancient civilizations adored "God the Mother" within the most profound part of our Being. The feminine principle of the Eternal One is Isis, Mary, Tonantzin, Cybele, Rhea, Adonia, Insoberta, etc.

If in our merely physical aspect we have a father and a mother, likewise within the deepest part of our Being we also have our Father who is in secret, as well as our Divine Mother Kundalini.

There are as many Fathers in Heaven as there are humans on Earth. God the Mother within our own intimacy is the feminine aspect of our Father who dwells in secret.

He and she are certainly the two superior parts of our inner Being.

Undoubtedly, he and she are our very true Being, beyond the "I" of psychology.

He unfolds into her. He commands, directs, instructs. She eliminates the undesirable elements that we carry in our interior with the condition that we continuously work on ourselves.

Thus, when we have died radically, when all the undesirable elements have been eliminated, after many conscious labors and voluntary sufferings, then we

shall fuse and integrate ourselves with
our "Father-Mother." Then, we shall be
terrifically divine gods, beyond good and
evil.

Any of those "I's" that have been previously observed and judged can be reduced
to cosmic dust by means of the fiery
powers of our own individual, particular
Divine Mother.

A specific formula in order to pray to
our inner Divine Mother is not necessary.
We must be very natural and simple when
we address her. The child who addresses
their mother never has a special formula.
The child utters what comes from their
heart, and that is all.

No "I" is instantaneously dissolved.
Our Divine Mother must work and even
suffer very much before achieving the
annihilation of any "I."

Make yourselves introversive, direct
your prayer within, seeking within your
interior your Divine Lady. Thus, with
sincere supplications, you shall be able
to talk to her. Beg her to disintegrate the
"I" that you have previously observed and
judged.

As the sense of self-observation develops, it shall permit you to verify the progressive advancement of your work.

Comprehension and discernment are fundamental. Nonetheless, something more is necessary if indeed we want to disintegrate the "myself."

The mind can give onto itself the luxury of labeling any defect, passing it from one department to the other, exhibiting it, hiding it, etc. However, the mind can never fundamentally alter the defect.

A special power superior to the mind is necessary, a fiery power that is capable of reducing any defect to ashes.

Stella Maris, our Divine Mother, has that power. She is able to pulverize any psychological defect.

Our Divine Mother lives in our intimacy, beyond the body, affections and the mind. She is, by herself, an igneous power superior to the mind.

Our own particular, individual Cosmic Mother possesses wisdom, love, and power. Within her is absolute perfection.

Good intentions and their constant repetition lead nowhere. These are good for nothing. It serves no purpose to repeat, "I will not be lustful," because within the very depth of our psyche, the "I's" of lasciviousness will continue to exist anyway.

It is useless to repeat daily, "I will not have anger," because within our psychological depths the "I's" of anger will continue to exist.

It would be useless to repeat daily, "I will no longer be covetous," because within the different depths of our psyche, the "I's" of covetousness shall continue to exist.

It would be useless to separate ourselves from the world and lock ourselves up in a convent or live in a cavern, because the "I's" within us will continue to exist.

Some hermits who isolated themselves within caves, based on rigorous disciplines, attained the ecstasy of the saints and were taken up to heaven. There they saw and heard things that are not easily comprehended by human beings. Nevertheless, their "I's" continued to exist within their interior.

Unquestionably, the Essence, through rigorous discipline, can escape from within the "I"; thus, it enjoys ecstasy. However, after such bliss, the Essence returns into the interior of the "myself."

Those who have become accustomed to ecstasy without having dissolved the ego believe that they have already reached liberation. They fool themselves by believing themselves to be masters. They even enter into the submerged devolution.

Nonetheless, we are not pronouncing ourselves against mystical ecstasy, against the ecstasy and happiness of the soul while in the absence of the ego. We only want to place emphasis on the necessity of dissolving "I's" in order to achieve the final liberation.

The Essence of any disciplined hermit, accustomed to escaping from within the "I," repeats such a feat after the death of his physical body. Then, his Essence enjoys the ecstasy for some time. Yet, after such time, his Essence returns as the Genie of Aladdin's lamp, back into the interior of the lamp, the ego, the myself.

Thereupon, he has no other choice but to return into a new physical body with the purpose of repeating his life on the stage of existence.

Many mystics who lived and died in the caverns of the Himalayas in central

Asia reincarnated again and are now vulgar, common, and current people in this world, in spite of the fact that their followers still adore and venerate them.

Therefore, any attempt at liberation, no matter how great it might be, if it does not take into consideration the necessity of dissolving the ego, it is condemned to failure.

Glossary

Centers: The human being has seven centers of psychological activity. The first five are the Intellectual, Emotional, Motor, Instinctive, and Sexual Centers. However, through inner development one learns how to utilize the Superior Emotional and Superior Intellectual Centers. Most people do not use these two at all.

The seven centers are also referred to as three centers: Intellectual, Emotional, and Motor-Instinctive-Sexual.

Chakra: (Sanskrit) Literally, "wheel." The chakras are subtle centers of energetic transformation. There are hundreds of chakras in our multi-dimensional physiology, but seven primary ones related to the awakening of consciousness.

"The chakras are points of connection through which the divine energy circulates from one to another vehicle of the human being." —Samael Aun Weor, *Aztec Christic Magic*

Christ: Derived from the Greek Christos, "the Anointed One," and Krestos, whose esoteric meaning is "fire." The word Christ is a title, not a personal name.

There is only one cosmic religion. Periodically, it is brought to us to help us out of the darkness; that is how each religion began. Since all religions are manifestataions of the one root religion, Christ is the basis of every religion. Each religion has their own symbols and names for Christ.

- In Hinduism, Christ is symbolized as Vishnu, who sends his avatars (incarnations, bodhisattvas) to the world to establish dharma. Krishna, Babaji, Rama, Sri Shankaracharya, and many others incarnated Christ.

- In Buddhism, Christ is Avalokitesvara, Chenresig, 觀世音 Guānshìyīn ("who perceives the world's lamentations"), the power of compassion and sacrifice for others, which manifests as Tara, and is harnessed within us by means of bodhichitta.

- Among the Persians, Christ is Ormuz, Ahura Mazda, the terrible enemy of Ahriman (Satan), which we carry within us.

- Among the Egyptians, Christ is Osiris and whosoever incarnated him was Osirified.

- Among the Chinese, the Cosmic Christ is Fu Xi (伏羲), who composed the I-Ching (The Book of Laws).

- Among the Greeks, Christ is symbolized in many ways: Zeus (Jupiter, the Father of the Gods), Apollo, Heracles, etc.

- Among the Aztecs, Christ is Quetzalcoatl.

- In the Germanic Edda, Baldur is the Christ who was assassinated by Hodur, god of war, with an arrow made from a twig of mistletoe.

"Indeed, Christ is a Sephirothic Crown (Kether, Chokmah and Binah) of incommensurable wisdom, whose purest atoms shine within Chokmah, the world of the Ophanim. Christ is not the Monad, Christ is not the Theosophical septenary; Christ is not the Jivan-Atman. Christ is the Central Sun. Christ is the ray that unites us to the Absolute." —Samael Aun Weor, *Tarot and Kabbalah*

"The Gnostic Church adores the Saviour of the World, Jesus. The Gnostic Church knows that Jesus incarnated Christ, and that is why they adore him. Christ is not a human nor a divine individual. Christ is a title given to all fully self-realised Masters. Christ is the Army of the Voice. Christ is the Verb. The Verb is far beyond the body, the soul and the Spirit. Everyone who is able to incarnate the Verb receives in fact the title of Christ. Christ is the Verb itself. It is necessary for everyone of us to incarnate the Verb (Word). When the Verb becomes flesh in us we speak with the verb of light. In actuality, several Masters have incarnated the Christ. In secret India, the Christ Yogi Babaji has lived for millions of years; Babaji is immortal. The great master of wisdom Kout Humi also incarnated the Christ. Sanat Kumara, the founder of the great College of Initiates of the White Lodge, is another living Christ. In the past, many incarnated the Christ. In the present, some have incarnated the Christ. In the future many will incarnate the Christ. John the Baptist also incarnated the Christ. John the Baptist is a living Christ. The difference between Jesus and the other Masters that also incarnated the Christ has to do with hierarchy. Jesus is the highest solar initiate of the Cosmos..." —Samael Aun Weor, *The Perfect Matrimony*

Consciousness: The modern English term consciousness is derived primarily from the Latin word conscius, "knowing, aware." Thus, consciousness is the basic factor of perception and understanding, and is therefore the basis of any living thing. Since living things are not equal and have a great deal of variety, so too does consciousness: it has infinite potential for development, either towards the heights of perfection or towards the depths of degeneration.

"Wherever there is life, there is consciousness. Consciousness is inherent to life as humidity is inherent to water." —Samael Aun Weor, *Sexology, the Basis of Endocrinology and Criminology*

"It is vital to understand and develop the conviction that consciousness has the potential to increase to an infinite degree." —The 14th Dalai Lama

"Light and consciousness are two phenomena of the same thing; to a lesser degree of consciousness, corresponds a lesser degree of light; to a greater degree of consciousness, a greater degree of light." —Samael Aun Weor, *The Esoteric Treatise of Hermetic Astrology*

Devolution: (Latin) From devolvere: backwards evolution, degeneration. The natural mechanical inclination for all matter and energy in nature to return towards their state of inert uniformity. Related to the Arcanum Ten: Retribution, the Wheel of Becoming. Devolution is the inverse process of evolution. As evolution is the complication of matter or energy, devolution is the slow process of nature to simplify matter or energy by applying forces to it. Through devolution, protoplasmic matter and energy descend, degrade, and increase in density within the infradimensions of nature to finally reach the center of the earth where they attain their ultimate state of inert uniformity. Devolution transfers the psyche, moral values, consciousness, or psychological responsibilities to inferior degradable organisms (Klipoth) through the surrendering of our psychological values to animal behaviors, especially sexual degeneration.

Divine Mother: The Divine Mother is the eternal, feminine principle, which is formless, and further unfolds into many levels, aspects, and manifestations.

"Devi or Sakti is the Mother of Nature. She is Nature Itself. The whole world is Her body. Mountains are Her bones. Rivers are Her veins. Ocean is Her bladder. Sun, moon are Her eyes. Wind is Her breath. Agni is Her mouth. She runs this world show. Sakti is symbolically female; but It is, in reality, neither male nor female. It is only a Force which manifests Itself in various forms. The five elements and their combinations are the external manifestations of the Mother. Intelligence, discrimination, psychic power, and will are Her internal manifestations." —Swami Sivananda

"Among the Aztecs, she was known as Tonantzin, among the Greeks as chaste Diana. In Egypt she was Isis, the Divine Mother, whose veil no mortal has lifted. There is no doubt at all that esoteric Christianity has never forsaken the worship of the Divine Mother Kundalini. Obviously she is Marah, or better said, RAM-IO, MARY. What orthodox religions did not specify, at least with regard to the exoteric or public circle, is the aspect of Isis in her individual human form. Clearly, it was taught only in secret to the Initiates that this Divine Mother exists individually within each human being. It cannot be emphasized enough that Mother-God, Rhea, Cybele, Adonia, or whatever we wish to call her, is a variant of our own individual Being in the here and now. Stated explicitly, each of us has our own particular, individual Divine Mother." —Samael Aun Weor, *The Great Rebellion*

"Devi Kundalini, the Consecrated Queen of Shiva, our personal Divine Cosmic Individual Mother, assumes five transcendental mystic aspects in every creature, which we must enumerate:

1. The unmanifested Prakriti

2. The chaste Diana, Isis, Tonantzin, Maria or better said Ram-Io

3. The terrible Hecate, Persephone, Coatlicue, queen of the infernos and death; terror of love and law

4. The special individual Mother Nature, creator and architect of our physical organism

5. The Elemental Enchantress to whom we owe every vital impulse, every instinct." —Samael Aun Weor, *The Secret of the Golden Flower*

Ego: The multiplicity of contradictory psychological elements that we have inside are in their sum the "ego." Each one is also called "an ego" or an "I." Every ego is a psychological defect which produces suffering. The ego is three (related to our three brains or three centers of psychological processing), seven (capital sins), and legion (in their infinite variations).

"The ego is the root of ignorance and pain." — Samael Aun Weor, *The Esoteric Treatise of Hermetic Astrology*

"The Being and the ego are incompatible. The Being and the ego are like water and oil. They can never be mixed... The annihilation of the psychic aggregates (egos) can be made possible only by radically comprehending our errors through meditation and by the evident Self-reflection of the Being." —Samael Aun Weor, *The Gnostic Bible: The Pistis Sophia Unveiled*

Essence: From the Chinese ⊠ ti, which literally means "substance, body" and is often translated as "essence," to indicate that which is always there throughout transformations. In gnosis, the term essence refers to our consciousness, which remains fundamentally the same, in spite of the many transformations it suffers, especially life, death, and being trapped in psychological defects. A common example given in Buddhism is a glass of water: even if filled with dirt and impurities, the water is still there. However, one would not want to drink it that way. Just so with the Essence (the consciousness): our Essence is trapped in impurities; to use it properly, it must be cleaned first.

"Singularly radiating is the wondrous Light;
Free is it from the bondage of matter and the senses.
Not binding by words and letters.
The Essence [⊠] is nakedly exposed in its pure eternity.
Never defiled is the Mind-nature;
It exists in perfection from the very beginning.
By merely casting away your delusions
The Suchness of Buddhahood is realized."
— Shen Tsan

"Zen, however, is interested not in these different "fields" but only in penetrating to ☒ the Essence, or the innermost core of the mind for it holds that once this core is grasped, all else will become relatively insignificant, and crystal clear... only by transcending [attachment] may one come to the innermost core of Mind—the perfectly free and thoroughly nonsubstantial illuminating-Voidness. This illuminating-Void character, empty yet dynamic, is the Essence (Chinese: ☒ ti) of the mind... The Essence of mind is the Illuminating-Void Suchness."
-G.C.Chang, *The Practice of Zen* (1959)

"Without question the Essence, or consciousness, which is the same thing, sleeps deeply... The Essence in itself is very beautiful. It came from above, from the stars. Lamentably, it is smothered deep within all these "I's" we carry inside. By contrast, the Essence can retrace its steps, return to the point of origin, go back to the stars, but first it must liberate itself from its evil companions, who have trapped it within the slums of perdition. Human beings have three percent free Essence, and the other ninety-seven percent is imprisoned within the "I's"." —Samael Aun Weor, *The Great Rebellion*

"A percentage of psychic Essence is liberated when a defect is disintegrated. Thus, the psychic Essence which is bottled up within our defects will be completely liberated when we disintegrate each and every one of our false values, in other words, our defects. Thus, the radical transformation of ourselves will occur when the totality of our Essence is liberated. Then, in that precise moment, the eternal values of the Being will express themselves through us. Unquestionably, this would be marvelous not only for us, but also for all of humanity." —Samael Aun Weor, *The Revolution of the Dialectic*

Evolution: "It is not possible for the true human being (the Self-realized Being) to appear through the mechanics of evolution. We know very well that evolution and its twin sister devolution are nothing else but two laws which constitute the mechanical axis of all Nature. One evolves to a certain perfectly defined point, and then the de-volving process follows. Every ascent is followed by a descent and vice-versa." —Samael Aun Weor, *Treatise of Revolutionary Psychology*.

"Evolution is a process of complication of en-ergy." —Samael Aun Weor, *The Perfect Matrimony*

Gnosis: (Greek) Knowledge.

1. The word Gnosis refers to the knowledge we acquire through our own experience, as opposed to knowledge that we are told or believe in. Gnosis - by whatever name in history or culture - is conscious, experiential knowledge, not merely intellectual or conceptual knowledge, belief, or theory. This term is synonymous with the Hebrew "daath" and the Sanskrit "jna."

2. The tradition that embodies the core wisdom or knowledge of humanity.

"Gnosis is the flame from which all religions sprouted, because in its depth Gnosis is religion. The word "religion" comes from the Latin word "religare," which implies "to link the Soul to God"; so Gnosis is the very pure flame from where all religions sprout, because Gnosis is knowledge, Gnosis is wisdom." —Samael Aun Weor from the lecture entitled The Esoteric Path

"The secret science of the Sufis and of the Whirling Dervishes is within Gnosis. The secret doctrine of Buddhism and of Taoism is within Gnosis. The sacred magic of the Nordics is within Gnosis. The wisdom of Hermes, Buddha, Confucius, Mohammed and Quetzalcoatl, etc., etc., is within Gnosis. Gnosis is the doctrine of Christ." —Samael Aun Weor, *The Revolution of Beelzebub*

Innermost: "Our real Being is of a universal nature. Our real Being is neither a kind of superior nor inferior "I." Our real Being is impersonal, universal, divine. He transcends every concept of "I," me, myself, ego, etc., etc." —Samael Aun Weor, *The Perfect Matrimony*

Also known as Atman, the Spirit, Chesed, our own individual interior divine Father.

"The Innermost is the ardent flame of Horeb. In accordance with Moses, the Innermost is the Ruach Elohim (the Spirit of God) who sowed the waters in the beginning of the world. He is the Sun King, our Divine Monad, the Alter-Ego of Cicerone." —Samael Aun Weor, *The Revolution of Beelzebub*

Intellectual Animal: When the Intelligent Principle, the Monad, sends its spark of consciousness into Nature, that spark, the anima, enters into manifestation as a simple mineral. Gradually, over millions of years, the anima gathers experience and evolves up the chain of life until it perfects itself in the level of the mineral kingdom. It then graduates into the plant kingdom, and subsequently into the animal kingdom. With each ascension the spark receives new capacities and higher grades of complexity. In the animal kingdom it learns procreation by ejaculation. When that animal intelligence enters into the human kingdom, it receives a new capacity: reasoning, the intellect; it is now an anima with intellect: an Intellectual Animal. That spark must then perfect itself in the human kingdom in order to become a complete and perfect human being, an entity that has conquered and transcended everything that belongs to the lower kingdoms. Unfortunately, very few intellectual animals perfect themselves; most remain enslaved by their animal nature, and thus are reabsorbed by Nature, a process belonging to the Devolving side of life and called by all the great religions "Hell" or the Second Death.

"The present manlike being is not yet human; he is merely an intellectual animal. It is a very grave error to call the legion of the "I" the "soul." In fact, what the manlike being has is the psychic material, the material for the soul within his Essence, but indeed, he does not have a Soul yet."
—Samael Aun Weor, *The Revolution of the Dialectic*

Internal Worlds: The many dimensions beyond the physical world. These dimensions are both subjective and objective. To know the objective internal worlds (the Astral Plane, or Nirvana, or the Klipoth) one must first know one's own personal, subjective internal worlds, because the two are intimately associated.

"Whosoever truly wants to know the internal worlds of the planet Earth or of the solar system or of the galaxy in which we live, must previously know his intimate world, his individual, internal life, his own internal worlds. Man, know thyself, and thou wilt know the universe and its gods. The more we explore this internal world called "myself," the more we will comprehend that we simultaneously live in two worlds, in two realities, in two confines: the external and the internal. In the same way that it is indispensable for one to learn how to walk in the external world so as not to fall down into a precipice, or not get lost in the streets of the city, or to select one's friends, or not associate with the perverse ones, or not eat poison, etc.; likewise, through the psychological work upon oneself we learn how to walk in the internal world, which is explorable only through Self-observation." —Samael Aun Weor, *Treatise of Revolutionary Psychology*

Through the work in Self-observation, we develop the capacity to awaken where previously we were asleep: including in the objective internal worlds.

Karma: (Sanskrit, literally "deed"; derived from kri, "to do...") The law of cause and effect.

"Be not deceived; God is not mocked: for whatsoever a man soweth, that shall he also reap." —Galatians 6:7

Kundalini: "Kundalini, the serpent power or mystic fire, is the primordial energy or Sakti that lies dormant or sleeping in the Muladhara Chakra, the centre of the body. It is called the serpentine or annular power on account of serpentine form. It is an electric fiery occult power, the great pristine force which underlies all organic and inorganic matter. Kundalini is the cosmic

power in individual bodies. It is not a material
force like electricity, magnetism, centripetal or
centrifugal force. It is a spiritual potential Sakti
or cosmic power. In reality it has no form. [...]
O Divine Mother Kundalini, the Divine Cosmic
Energy that is hidden in men! Thou art Kali,
Durga, Adisakti, Rajarajeswari, Tripurasundari,
Maha-Lakshmi, Maha-Sarasvati! Thou hast put
on all these names and forms. Thou hast manifested as Prana, electricity, force, magnetism,
cohesion, gravitation in this universe. This whole
universe rests in Thy bosom. Crores of saluta-
tions unto thee. O Mother of this world! Lead
me on to open the Sushumna Nadi and take
Thee along the Chakras to Sahasrara Chakra and
to merge myself in Thee and Thy consort, Lord
Siva. Kundalini Yoga is that Yoga which treats of
Kundalini Sakti, the six centres of spiritual energy (Shat Chakras), the arousing of the sleeping
Kundalini Sakti and its union with Lord Siva in
Sahasrara Chakra, at the crown of the head. This
is an exact science. This is also known as Laya
Yoga. The six centres are pierced (Chakra Bheda)
by the passing of Kundalini Sakti to the top of
the head. 'Kundala' means 'coiled'. Her form is
like a coiled serpent. Hence the name Kundalini." —Swami Sivananda, *Kundalini Yoga*

Logos: Greek, from lego "I say," means Verb or
Word. The unifying principle. The Logos is the
manifested deity of every nation and people; the
outward expression or the effect of the cause
which is ever concealed. (Speech is the "logos"
of thought). The Logos has three aspects, known
universally as the Trinity, Trikaya, or Trimurti.

These are related to the three primary forces behind all forms of creation.

Meditation: "When the esotericist submerges himself into meditation, what he seeks is information." —Samael Aun Weor

"It is urgent to know how to meditate in order to comprehend any psychic aggregate, or in other words, any psychological defect. It is indispensable to know how to work with all our heart and with all our soul, if we want the elimination to occur." —Samael Aun Weor, *The Gnostic Bible: The Pistis Sophia Unveiled*

"1. The Gnostic must first attain the ability to stop the course of his thoughts, the capacity to not think. Indeed, only the one who achieves that capacity will hear the Voice of the Silence.

"2. When the Gnostic disciple attains the capacity to not think, then he must learn to concentrate his thoughts on only one thing.

"3. The third step is correct meditation. This brings the first flashes of the new consciousness into the mind.

"4. The fourth step is contemplation, ecstasy or Samadhi. This is the state of Turiya (perfect clairvoyance). —Samael Aun Weor, *The Perfect Matrimony*

Personality: (Latin personae: mask) There are two fundamental types of personality:

1. Solar: the personality of the inner Being. This type is only revealed through the liberation of the mind from samsara.

2. Lunar: the terrestrial, perishable personality. We create a new lunar personality in the

first seven years of each new physical body, in accordance with three influences: genotype, phenotype and paratype. Genotype is the influence of the genes, or in other words, karma, our inheritance from past actions. Phenotype is the education we receive from our family, friends, teachers, etc. Paratype is related to the circumstances of life.

"The personality is time. The personality lives in its own time and does not reincarnate. After death, the personality also goes to the grave. For the personality there is no tomorrow. The personality lives in the cemetery, wanders about the cemetery or goes down into its grave. It is neither the Astral Body nor the ethereal double. It is not the Soul. It is time. It is energetic and it disintegrates very slowly. The personality can never reincarnate. It does not ever reincarnate. There is no tomorrow for the human personality." —Samael Aun Weor, *The Perfect Matrimony*

"The human personality is only a marionette controlled by invisible strings... Evidently, each one of these I's puts in our minds what we must think, in our mouths what we must say, and in our hearts what we must feel, etc. Under such conditions the human personality is no more than a robot governed by different people, each disputing its superiority and aspiring to supreme control of the major centers of the organic machine... First of all, it is necessary, urgent and imperative that the magnetic center, which is abnormally established in our false personality, be transferred to the Essence. In this way, the complete human can initiate his journey from the personality up to the stars, ascending in a progressive, didactic way, step by step up the Mountain of the Being. As long as the magnetic center continues to be established in our illusory personality we will live in the most abominable psychological dens of iniquity, although appearing to be splendid citizens in everyday life... These values which serve as a basis for the law of recurrence are always found within our human personality." —Samael Aun Weor, *The Great Rebellion*

"The personality must not be confused with the "I." In fact, the personality is formed during the first seven years of childhood. The "I" is something different. It is the error which is perpetuated from century to century; it fortifies itself each time, more and more through the mechanics of recurrence. The personality is energetic. It is born during infancy through habits, customs, ideas, etc., and it is fortified with the experiences of life. Therefore, both the personality as well as the "I" must be disintegrated. These psychological teachings are more revolutionary than those of Gurdjieff and Ouspensky. The "I" utilizes the personality as an instrument of action. Thus, personalism is a mixture of ego and personality. Personality worship was invented by the "I." In fact, personalism engenders egoism, hatred, violence, etc. All of this is rejected by ahimsa. Personality totally ruins esoteric organizations. Personality produces anarchy and confusion. Personalism can totally destroy any organization... The personality is multiple and has many hidden depths. The karma of previous existences is deposited into the personality. It is karma in the process of fulfillment or crystallization. The impressions which are not digested become new psychic aggregates, and what is more serious, they become new personalities. The personality is not homogenous but rather heterogeneous and plural. One must select impressions in the same manner that one chooses the things of life. If one forgets oneself at a given instant, in a new event, new "I's" are formed, and if they are very strong they become new personalities within the personality. Therein lies the cause of many traumas, complexes and psychological conflicts. An impression which one does not digest may form into a personality within the personality, and if one does not accept it, it becomes a source of frightening conflicts. Not all the personalities (which one carries within the personality) are accepted; the latter giving origin to many traumas, complexes, phobias, etc. Before all else, it is necessary to comprehend the multiplicity of the personality. The personality is multiple in itself. Therefore, there could be someone who may have disintegrated the psychic aggregates, but if he does not disintegrate the personality, he will not be able to attain authentic enlightenment and the joy of living." —Samael Aun Weor, *The Revolution of the Dialectic*

"The personality is energetic. The personality takes form during the first seven years of childhood and is strengthened with time and experiences... The Mental Body, the Body of Desires, the Ethereal Body, and the Physical Body integrate the personality... We must finish with the personality and with the "I" in order for the Being to be born within ourselves." —Samael Aun Weor, *Tarot and Kabbalah*

Self-observation: An exercise of attention, in which one learns to become an indifferent observer of one's own psychological process. True Self-observation is an active work of directed attention, without the interference of thought.

"We need attention intentionally directed towards the interior of our own selves. This is not a passive attention. Indeed, dynamic attention proceeds from the side of the observer, while thoughts and emotions belong to the side which is observed." —Samael Aun Weor, *Treatise of Revolutionary Psychology*

Self-realization: The achievement of perfect knowledge. This phrase is better stated as, "The realization of the Innermost Self," or "The realization of the true nature of self." At the ultimate level, this is the experiential, conscious knowledge of the Absolute, which is synonymous with Emptiness, Shunyata, or Non-being.

Self-remembering: A state of active consciousness, controlled by will, that begins with awareness of being here and now. This state has many levels (see: Consciousness). True Self-remembering occurs without thought or mental processing: it is a state of conscious perception and includes the remembrance of the inner Being.

Solar Human: A human being who has created the soul. As Jesus taught, "With patience ye shall possess thy soul" [Luke 21:19]. Just as the physical body establish our basis for existence in the physical world, there are bodies that establish our existence in the superior worlds ("heaven"). Jesus explained this as the second birth (John 3), and are called solar bodies. These bodies or vehicles are superior due to being created from Solar (Christic) energy (i.e. the "light of the world," the "Sun"), as opposed to the inferior, lunar bodies we receive from nature. Together, they are called "the soul," and are also known as the Wedding Garment (Christianity), the Merkabah (Kabbalah), To Soma Heliakon (Greek), and Sahu (Egyptian). The method to create these bodies was veiled in the traditions of Tantra and Alchemy.

"All the masters of the White Lodge, the Angels, Archangels, Thrones, Seraphim, Virtues, etc., etc., etc. are garbed with the solar bodies. Only those who have solar bodies have the Being incarnated. Only someone who possesses the Being is an authentic human being." —Samael Aun Weor, *The Esoteric Treatise of Hermetic Astrology*

Subjective: "What do modern psychologists understand as 'objective?' They understand it to be that which is external to the mind: the physical, the tangible, the material.

"Yet, they are totally mistaken, because when analysing the term "subjective," we see that it signifies "sub, under," that which is below the range of our perceptions. What is below our perceptions? Is it not perhaps the infernal worlds? Is it not perhaps subjective that which is in the physical or beneath the physical? So, what is truly subjective is what is below the limits of our perceptions.

"Psychologists do not know how to use the former terms correctly.

"Objective: the light, the resplendence; it is that which contains the Truth, clarity, lucidity.

"Subjective: the darkness, the tenebrous. The subjective elements of perception are the outcome of seeing, hearing, touching, smelling and tasting. All of these are perceptions of what we see in the third dimension. For example, in one cube we see only length, width and height. We do not see the fourth dimension because we are bottled up within the ego. The subjective elements of perception are constituted by the ego with all of its "I's." —Samael Aun Weor, *Tarot and Kabbalah*

White Fraternity, Lodge, or Brotherhood: That ancient collection of pure souls who maintain the highest and most sacred of sciences: White Magic or White Tantra. It is called White due to its purity and cleanliness. This "Brotherhood" or "Lodge" includes human beings of the highest order from every race, culture, creed and religion, and of both sexes.

Index

About the Author

His name is Hebrew סמאל און ואור, and is pronounced "sam-ayel on vay-or." You may not have heard of him, but Samael Aun Weor changed the world.

In 1950, in his first two books, he became the first person to reveal the esoteric secret hidden in all the world's great religions, and for that, accused of "healing the ill," he was put in prison. Nevertheless, he did not stop. Between 1950 and 1977 — merely twenty-seven years — not only did Samael Aun Weor write over sixty books on the most difficult subjects in the world, such as consciousness, kabbalah, physics, tantra, meditation, etc., in which he deftly exposed the singular root of all knowledge — which he called Gnosis — he simultaneously inspired millions of people across the entire span of Latin America: stretching across twenty countries and an area of more than 21,000,000 square kilometers, founding schools everywhere, even in places without electricity or post offices.

During those twenty-seven years, he experienced all the extremes that humanity could give him, from adoration to death threats, and in spite of the enormous popularity of his books and lectures, he renounced an income, refused recognitions, walked away from accolades, and consistently turned away those who would worship him. He held as friends both presidents and peasants, and yet remained a mystery to all.

When one reflects on the effort and will it requires to perform even day to day tasks, it is astonishing to consider the herculean efforts required to accomplish what he did in such a short time. But, there is a reason: he was a man who knew who he was, and what he had to do. A true example of compassion and selfless service, Samael Aun Weor dedicated the whole of his life to freely helping anyone and everyone find the path out of suffering. His mission was to show all of humanity the universal source of all spiritual traditions, which he did not only through his writings and lectures, but also through his actions. He said,

"I, the one who writes this book, am not anyone's master, and I beg people to not follow me. I am an imperfect human just like anyone else, and it is an error to follow someone who is imperfect. Let every one follow their "I am [their Innermost]...

"I do not want to receive visitors. Unquestionably, I am nothing more than a postman, a courier, a man that delivers a message... It would be the breaking point of silliness for you to come from your country to the capital city of Mexico with the only purpose of visiting a vulgar postman, an employee that delivered you a letter in the past... Why would you waste your money for that? Why would you visit a simple courier, a miserable postman? It is better for you to study the message, the written teachings delivered in the books...

"I have not come to form any sect, or one more belief, nor am I interested in the schools of today, or the particular beliefs of anyone! ...

"We are not interested in anyone's money, nor are we interested in monthly fees, or temples made out of brick, cement or clay, because we are conscious visitors in the cathedral of the soul and we know that wisdom is of the soul.

"Flattery tires us, praise should only belong to our Father (who is in secret and watches over us minutely).

"We are not in search of followers; all we want is for each person to follow his or her self—their own internal master, their sacred Innermost—because he is the only one who can save and glorify us.

"I do not follow anyone, therefore no one should follow me...

"We do not want any more comedies, pretenses, false mysticism, or false schools. What we want now are living realities; we want to prepare ourselves to see, hear, and touch the reality of those truths..."

—Samael Aun Weor

Your book reviews matter.

Glorian Publishing is a very small non-profit organization, thus we have no money to spend on marketing and advertising. Fortunately, there is a proven way to gain the attention of readers: book reviews. Mainstream book reviewers won't review these books, but you can.

The path of liberation requires the daily balance of three active factors:

- birth of virtue
- death of vice
- sacrifice for others

Writing book reviews is a powerful way to sacrifice for others. By writing book reviews on popular websites, you help to make the books more visible to humanity, and you might help save a soul from suffering. Will you do your part to help us show these wonderful teachings to others? Take a moment today to write a review.

Donate

Glorian Publishing is a non-profit publisher dedicated to spreading the sacred universal doctrine to suffering humanity. All of our works are made possible by the kindness and generosity of sponsors. If you would like to make a tax-deductible donation, you may send it to the address below, or visit our website for other alternatives. If you would like to sponsor the publication of a book, please contact us at (844) 945-6742 or help@glorian.org.

Glorian Publishing
PO Box 209
Clinton, CT 06413 US
Phone: (844) 945-6742
VISIT US ONLINE AT glorian.org